# VISUAL DISABILITY IN THE ELDERLY

# Visual Disability in the Elderly

TIM CULLINAN, MB, BChir, MSc, MD
Senior Lecturer
Department of Environmental and Preventive Medicine
The Medical College of St Bartholomew's Hospital
London

*with a chapter by* Janet Silver

CROOM HELM
London & Sydney

© 1986 Tim Cullinan
Croom Helm Ltd, Provident House, Burrell Row,
Beckenham, Kent BR3 1AT
Croom Helm Australia Pty Ltd, Suite 4, 6th Floor,
64–76 Kippax Street, Surry Hills, NSW 2010 Australia

British Library Cataloguing in Publication Data

Cullinan, Tim
    Visual disability in the elderly.
    1. Aged, visually handicapped
    I. Title   II. Silver, Janet
    362.4′1′0880565      HV1597.5

ISBN 0–7099–3409–2

Distributed exclusively in the United States and non-exclusively in Canada,
Mexico, Central and South America, by:

PSG Publishing Company, Inc., Box 6, 545 Great Road, Littleton, Massachusetts
01460

ISBN: 0–88416–560–4

Printed and bound in Great Britain by
Biddles Ltd, Guildford and King's Lynn

# CONTENTS

# PREFACE

This book is about elderly people with poor sight, about their difficulties, about the causes of their poor sight and about how they might best be helped, both by those in day-to-day contact with them and by society at large. It is intended to be readable – and therefore, hopefully, read; but it is also intended to dispel some of the fears that exist in many people's minds when eye diseases are mentioned and to show how much can be done by relatives, health and social workers, and non-specialist doctors to alleviate the inevitable plight of those who cannot see very well. I said 'can' be done – I mean 'must' be done, because if it is not done by those who have day-to-day contact with elderly people then it will often not be done at all. There are so many components to any disabling condition, especially if you are elderly or poor or both and so have limited opportunities to manipulate your environment, that comprehensive help is way beyond the realm of the specialist. It becomes, as perhaps it always should have been, a general responsibility and in order to shoulder it we all need under-standing. I hope this book will help.

# 1 VISUAL DISABILITY AND BLINDNESS

These title words bring to each of our minds a stereotyped picture of a 'blind' person which may well date back to our childhoods. Few of us know intimately anyone who is 'blind'; most of us rely, to a greater or lesser extent, on chance meetings we may have made and, perhaps, on the materials put out by the various agencies anxious to help different groups of blind people in need. To each of us, our own casual experience is valuable — it is the starting point on which true understanding can be built. But because it is seldom accurate it is usually of little use to those 'blind' individuals we are trying to help; and, if it is heavily coloured by our own unspoken fears or by unshakable beliefs in our own capacities, it may actually get in the way. This chapter will explore the various components of 'blindness' and 'visual disability' in relation to elderly people and to our understanding of their needs.

To be 'blind' is seldom to be in complete darkness. Less than one in 20 'blind' people, whatever their age, have no perception of light — almost all can orientate themselves, however imperfectly, using residual vision. This immediately introduces two concepts to the single idea of 'blindness' — what the individual is able to see, and what use he makes of that vision. The first, visual acuity, is usually measurable and, if its failure is dependent on a disease of the eye rather than the nerves and that part of the brain that supports it, can often be enhanced by optical and electronic aids, and by improvements in the physical environment. The second, visual ability, is much more determined by each person's hopes, fears, perceptions, personality and social surroundings. It too can be greatly enhanced with sensitive help.

Because visual acuity is relatively easy to measure, it has been used traditionally in statutory definitions of 'blindness', which are, of course, no more than a convenient administrative method of sorting out who supposedly needs, and who supposedly does not, the 'benefits' that society is prepared to offer. In many western countries visual acuity is the only criterion of blindness, though in Britain there is a flavour of 'visual ability' as well.* Basically, to become registered as blind in Britain, a person must be 'so blind as to be unable to perform any work for which eyesight is essential'[1] though, in implementing this, anyone with a visual acuity of less than 6/60 (that is, who cannot read the top line of the standard optician's chart) may be considered for registration as 'blind'. There is a gentle tautology in using the word 'blind' in a definition of 'blindness' but, apart from that, the whole thrust of the definition is towards younger, economically active people and, indeed, smacks a little of Poor Law labelling. The definition serves the elderly badly, in part because it concerns 'work' only and in part because it omits (as do all national definitions) any idea of 'near' rather than 'distance' vision (see Chapter 3). It is on 'near' vision that many components of elderly people's lives depend, especially if they are housebound.

The definition was first adopted in 1921 in a desire to bring educational and training facilities, and some economic relief, to those who needed it.[2] Before then, provision for both children and adults had been voluntary and many of the local societies engaged in helping the 'blind' were enlisted in the process of registration and, to an extent, remain so today. Judgements about who should or should not be registered must be made by a specialist ophthalmologist who examines the candidate and completes a form BD8 which he then sends to the local authority. Here the registers are kept. Anyone can refer himself to the specialist appointed by the local authority, or indeed refer anyone else; it does not have to be another doctor, though it usually is.

The benefits in becoming registered as 'blind' have changed over the years but currently (1985) include:
1. Increased income tax allowances;
2. Added supplementary benefits (to those already receiving them);
3. A special 'blind' pension;
4. Reduced rates for council house tenants;
5. Reduced or even free travel in many parts of the UK (with, sometimes, an escort);

---

* In countries where the means for measuring visual acuity are not universally available, visual ability may be the only criterion. Thus, in Zambia the definition of 'blindness' is 'an inability to move about in unfamiliar surroundings unaided, such aid including the blind man's stick'.[3]

6. A reduced TV licence (somewhat surprisingly);
7. Tuition in Braille or Moon (free);
8. Access to talking books (free);
9. Instruction in the use of a long cane (free);
10. For children there is also access to special education.

In 1948[1] a second category of partial sight was introduced in recognition of the many people with real sight difficulties who were excluded from help by the rigorous definition of 'blindness'. There never has been a statutory definition of partial sight, as there is for 'blindness', though it was suggested that those with a visual acuity of no more than 6/60 (the first line of the chart) should become eligible for entry on a partial sight register. They do not receive any of the financial benefits available to those registered as 'blind' but they are supposed to have the help of a specialist social worker. Unfortunately, social workers do not any longer have the specialist functions they used to have and many parts of the country, though not all, have lost those who concentrated solely on the 'blind'. Consequently, many elderly people fail to see any advantages in becoming registered as 'partially sighted'.

Finally, in both the definition of 'blind' and in the suggested criteria for 'partial sight', there is a place for those who retain adequate central sight, yet whose field of vision is so restricted that they are handicapped by it. Not more than 7 to 10 per cent of people on the 'blind' register, however, are there because of reduced fields alone.

So much for definitions and guidelines; they are no more than the devices by which society attempts to make itself manageable to those it decides cannot manage by themselves. Definitions are a gateway to 'benefits' — 'benefits' that may or may not seem adequate or appropriate either to the giver or the receiver. But to pass through the gateway implies 'costs'; to become registered is to accept the label 'blind', to come to terms with the fact that you are no longer in the sighted world and that, from now on, others are going to view you as someone apart, separate, demanding from them different responses and attitudes to those they would normally hold.

It is amazing how many of those 'costs' are actually bound up in the word 'blind' itself — it engenders in us all some sort of stereotyped response that has much to do with our own misgivings and experiences and little to do with the real needs of anyone we encounter who is labelled 'blind'. Moreover, our responses and attitudes can very well make life harder for a blind person than it need be — as Helen Kellar has put it: 'Not blindness, but the attitude of the seeing to the blind is the hardest burden to bear'.[4] A large literature has been built up round this whole process of becoming stigmatised and the part that the actual loss of sight, and of normally-sighted people's reactions, play in it; it has been well reviewed by Kemp.[5] However, most of the literature deals either with childhood development[6] or with the experiences of those who became 'blind' during their economically active years.[7] There is little enough on the elderly, who often have the added burden of other handicaps and far less opportunity to manipulate their environment and so to mitigate in some way the 'social distance' imposed by visual loss and by other people's attitudes to it. It has always been towards the young 'blind' that most attention, both in understanding and technology, has been directed; despite their tremendous burdens, the benefits to them in becoming 'labelled' may still greatly outweigh the costs.

But not so to the elderly who have to accept other people's stereotyped reactions to an equal degree, and yet gain fewer benefits. To them, the balance of the equation is often reversed and the 'costs' become paramount, whether they are related to other people, to self, or to the protective family or carer. The first has been extensively explored in the literature in relation to chance encounters — the waiter in the restaurant, the stranger in the street — where they undoubtedly occur most vividly. But they also occur in the attitudes and reactions of people much nearer and dearer. The sheer weariness of dealing daily with other people's inappropriate responses must be awe-inspiring to a younger 'blind' person; to an elderly one, it may well be the difference between going out and staying at home.

Yet to reject the 'label' may be even worse — to deny your blindness, not to use the white stick or the dark glasses that society demands of you, and yet to peer at price labels, fumble for change, stumble in the street invites judgements that have nothing to do with poor vision. You are senile, incompetent or attention-seeking, nothing but a nuisance, and quite unfit to be out on your own.

The costs to 'self' are equally high. There is the personal stereotype of blindness to be overcome — the 'spoiled identity' it implies — which means to the elderly, almost inevitably, acceptance of being old. The idea of a 'damaged self-image' is no less poignant in later life than it is at any other time: many elderly people deny 'blindness' or any significant visual difficulty for this reason alone,[8] without counting the social 'costs' already mentioned. This is especially so for those who have some other crippling disability with which to contend.[8]

The third element of 'costs' concerns those that the family or the carers have to pay for looking after a handicapped person. Hilbourne has written interestingly about it in relation to the 'blind'[9] — though it applies equally well to other situations. There are, of course, 'costs' in lost opportunities and restricted activities for those with someone to care for but there is also a 'courtesy stigma' as well. The caring person is no longer judged for himself, or more often herself, alone; she becomes assessed, criticised, even extravagantly praised for her ability to respond to the supposed needs of the handicapped person she is caring for. She herself becomes 'stigmatised' — and her perfectly natural reaction to this insidious and often pernicious process may be to change her way of filling her caring role.

Given all this, it is a small wonder that so many elderly people with profound sight difficulties are reluctant to admit it; and small wonder that there is a strong move to get rid of the value laden term 'blind' altogether. But these aspects of costs and benefits have been touched on here only to illustrate the conceptual deficiencies in any statutory definition of blindness — they will become more real in later chapters that deal with the difficulties of poorly sighted elderly people and the many ways in which those difficulties can be mitigated.

There is, however, another dimension in which any statutory definition of a disability must be examined, and that is how efficient it is at determining who is in need of the benefits it gives access to, and who is not. In a sense, it is a way of rationing limited resources and it explicitly excludes from those resources all who cannot meet its rigorous standards; declaring, if only implicitly, that they do not have similar needs to those who can. Yet it has been shown repeatedly that there are far more elderly people with lives handicapped by poor vision who do not meet the criteria for registration as blind or partially sighted, than who do,[8] and many of these would benefit greatly from what is offered to the registered. To this extent, the definition is exclusive; luckily, it appears to be rendered a little less so by the cheerful humanity of many ophthalmic specialists who are happy to temper the wind for the individual patient. The latest analyses of blind register data[10] shows that 25 per cent of elderly people become registered with a visual acuity which should have excluded them had the rules been applied strictly. There is much to be said for British compromise, even if it is too often in response to our own muddled thinking.

So on several counts it is wise to treat the word 'blind' with extreme reserve (though it remains a tremendous fund-raiser for just the reasons mentioned above). In an effort to side-step the concept and to incorporate the very many different definitions in use around the world, WHO devised in 1973 a classification of visual impairment* which has much to recommend it. It views visual impairment as a continuum reaching down in five measurable stages from a visual acuity of 6/24 (the third line in the standard chart) to no light perception at all. This is a much more liberal cut-off point than in any current national definition of 'blind' or even 'partial sight' and it has been shown that no-one, at least among the elderly, with distance vision better than this, identifies himself as having any serious sight problems.[8] There is, though, still a dependence on distance acuity alone (and visual fields), and not near vision which might be more appropriate for the elderly.

The chances of Britain or any other country rushing to adopt the WHO criteria as a means of delivering help are very slim. The floodgates of need, if not of demand, would be opened and both statutory and voluntary services overwhelmed. Besides which, the present definition of 'blind' is enshrined in an Act of Parliament[2] — it would take another Act to shatter the temple. But there is no reason why the WHO criteria should not be used by those having day-to-day care of elderly people as a conceptual framework around which they can assess individual needs, as well as for its original purpose of gathering comparable epidemiological data between countries.

---

*Strictly speaking, visual disability would be a more correct description; there is some 'impairment' of the optical system that confers a 'disability' on sight. Handicap implies that such a disability actually affects some aspect of living.[11]

## Attitudes and Needs

Blindness has always proved attractive to poets, playwrights and philosophers; dispense with one critical faculty, and you can enlarge almost endlessly on the sensibilities of the others. But to do so successfully, blindness must be absolute and explicit and it must be associated with a character who supposedly has something to give. The blind matchgirl, the minstrel, even the old blind bard all reach out to the sighted society in which they live in ways that can be easily understood and dramatised, and it is on these that our childhood stereotypes of 'blindness' depend. It is much harder for us to relate to the needs and difficulties of the poorly sighted, but far from 'blind', elderly people trying to thrive in a complex and modern society — we have no steroptype and even if we did it would probably be useless, if not actively destructive.

Latterly, of course, psychologists and sociologists have taken over from the poets and novelists and have endeavoured to provide frameworks around which understanding can be enhanced. They have taken three main directions: the perceptions, responses and adjustments that visually disabled people make in order to function in a sighted society; the responses that members of the society make to them; and the physical and social support necessary to make life tolerable. They have sought, reasonably, to discover generalities that adequately explain the behaviour of individuals and they have developed paradigms that have considerably advanced understanding — at least in a fairly narrow field of their own choosing.

At the same time, however, they have limited themselves largely to a young population of self-declared 'blind' people and have almost totally excluded the elderly — as Siller[12] says 'the larger population of blind persons has been abandoned in favour of the young' — to say nothing of those who have not declared themselves as 'blind', yet have great difficulty in seeing. It is easy to see why this is so. To study subjects who have at least acceptance of the label 'blind' in common, provides the researcher with a firm theoretical starting point; to deal with young, articulate people with a single handicap is much easier than to explore the difficulties of the old with multi-faceted difficulties, and to challenge and change stereotypes is far easier than to build models of understanding which are probably not to be generalised anyway. Moreover, the needs of the young are dynamic, be they educational or occupational, and have long been a thorn in the side of complacent societies to which they can easily and fairly cheaply respond. And, lastly, much of the research has been done by young PhD students with limited time and resources who find it much easier to take their subjects from some handy 'blind' register than to go out and seek in society for those groping their way towards the acceptance of such a generally approved label.

Nevertheless, much useful work has been done and although the application of models developed from studies of young, resilient 'blind' people to older people suffering from failing vision is hazardous in the extreme, a brief review of the field will aid an individual understanding of what may be going on between society, its sighted members and those elderly visually disabled people they are seeking to help.

## Self-perception

One of the strongest fields of research has been into how 'blind' people perceive themselves, their disability and the reaction of others to it. Perhaps the most useful model has been that of 'loss'; any life-diminishing event can be portrayed in terms of initial disbelief and denial followed by protest, depression and eventual acceptance. It is a model used by Fitzgerald[13] in a perceptive study of 66 newly registered blind people in London, and by Keegan, Ash and Greenaugh of 114 in Canada.[14] Both studies involved at least a few elderly people and showed that for them, as for others, full use of such social and technological help as was available came only with final acceptance of being 'blind'. It was those still going through a process of 'denial' or hoping for some sort of miracle cure who were presently beyond the reach of rehabilitation.

It is easy to believe that such statements might apply equally to elderly people, even with lesser loss of sight but it must be remembered they were made of subjects to whom sight loss was the only significant disability. Presumably it is harder to apply them when the slow deterioration of a crucial faculty may be only one facet of a long and lonely ageing process. Here it may be that perceptions of age rather than sight loss or any other disability play the greater part in determining successful adjustment. For example, Hicks [15] shows how chronic conditions tend to become gradually incorporated into a person's identification of self and thus become normal 'health'. Calnan[16] develops the idea further and speculates that since poor vision is one of the commonest attributes that elderly people identify as an age indicator, it can even take on a positive quality in that it attracts sympathy and help. In this context, to actively seek alleviation of the disability may imply losing these valued advantages, which may partially explain why so many old people quickly discard the aids that someone else has felt appropriate for them.[17] However that may be, it presumably all adds up to some sort of 'acceptance', even if not within the meaning of the word developed round the younger, resilient and truly 'blind' people.

Calnan[16] also refers to the 'health optimism' of old age that enables many old people to view themselves as lucky exceptions to the otherwise dreary rule of diminishing faculties and eventual death. To seek help for failing vision would be, in this sense, to become associated with all the other stereotypes of old age and literally the 'beginning of the end'. Nobody listening to one old person describing the problems of another can be anything but struck by how disability is dwelt upon, implicitly boosting the fitness of the other. To damage such optimism seems wrong, even if it is far from 'acceptance'; indeed, it may even be realistic, if only temporarily so, if it enables an elderly person to so circumscribe her own life in the face of diminishing faculties that they cease to limit what she wants to do.

But most eye disease in old age is progressive, and a time is usually reached when the limitations it imposes threaten treasured independence and it is then that sensitive help is needed even if it is not actively sought. At that point it behoves the helper to understand precisely what level of 'acceptance' has been achieved and in what terms, and not to rely on some catch-all care model that is almost certainly inappropriate to the needs and the self-perceptions of the individual.

## Attitudes of Others

As for the self-perceptions of the 'blind', most of the large amount of research that has attempted to analyse the responses of a sighted society to its sightless members has taken labelled 'blindness' as its starting point. Moreover, much of it has assumed that the 'blind' remain immutable in face of the responses they evoke in others — that a response pattern is a one-way thing. Indeed, earlier researchers such as Lukoff and Whiteman[18] are quoted by Kemp[19] as claiming that there is 'reasonable agreement by sighted people that blindness enables people to understand other persons, particularly if they are suffering; that the cues blind people receive are more readily translated into accurate perceptions; that the blind are not especially prone to un-happiness, resentment or mental illness and that blind persons are more sensitive to music and literature'. Such a direct, if muted, extension of childhood beliefs into the realms of social-psychology may be much to the purpose of (indeed even reinforced by) fund-raisers anxious to provide for neatly defined groups of young, potentially active people, but they do not fit most people's perceptions about elderly people with failing vision.

Luckily, however, even consistent attitudes to disability do not necessarily get translated into consistent behaviour and later studies have shown them anyway to be the exception rather than the rule. Delafield[20] has provided good evidence that while 'early studies on sighted attitudes to the blind seemed to suggest that there was a unitary dimension which might be discoverable . . . recent studies (he cites Siller[12]) have shown that sighted attitudes are neither consistent nor pervasive.'

That, presumably, is just as well because, while a fit and active 'blind' person may find it possible to fight his way through the inappropriate 'labels' and 'responses' that others attach to him, it is much more difficult for an elderly, multiply disabled person to do so. Indeed, the last thing anyone seeking to help such a person needs is a set of preconceived notions stemming from her own life-experiences and those of the society that influences them. Already the attitude of the young to the old in a modern society is counterproductive enough — Armstrong[21] has characterised it as 'negative' and claims with some justification that this has been reinforced by grouping the health problems of elderly people into a specialism of 'geriatric medicine', thus reinforcing the concept of multifaceted disease with a hopeless prognosis. All health prob-lems suffered by someone who is old tend to be drawn into 'the same depressing disease concept'[16] — thus lowering expectations both in the provider and recipient of care.

Against this background — and the manifest inability of any society to cope with all the problems posed by the degenerative diseases of old age — accurate assessment of what is and what is

not practicable for the relief of specific disabilites is hard to make
and old people tend to become typified by a major disability which
leaves other disabilities, perhaps amenable to treatment, unsought
and unrelieved. It is not surprising, then, that most professionals
having institutional care of the elderly are as unaware of who can
and cannot see well[22,23] as those in the community[8] — let alone
how relatively easy it often is to do something about it.[16] It
behoves all who have care of individual people, with or without
poor vision, to be aware of their personal perceptions of old age
and disability; and especially those professionals — opticians,
ophthalmologists, social workers, family doctors and occupational
therapists — whose job it is to chart an elderly person's journey
through the many stages of a progressively disabling disease
towards the eventual acceptance which will alone make life
tolerable and even enjoyable.

## Discovering Needs

Attempts to paint pictures of how visually disabled people
function socially and economically in modern society have either
been made with the broad brush of general disability or, once
again, from the too-narrow stance of the registered 'blind'. For the
elderly, neither attempt has been particularly successful, partly
because neither has paid much attention to the self-perceptions of
disabled people either in forming questions or analysing answers
and partly because of a too-ready tendency to ascribe all life's daily
difficulties to a single defined disability.

Collecting data on a survey basis is extremely expensive and to
be cost-effective must be as all-embracing as possible. This usually
leads to the inclusion of too few members of some smaller groups
to make any useful statements about their particular needs[8] and
visually handicapped people are always minority groups in gen-
eral-handicap surveys.[11] Whether, indeed, the collection of such
data has ever had any discernable influence on social policy, either
local or national, is open to debate.[24] It too often seems to become
an end in itself.

Nevertheless, some generally useful statements can be made.
Elderly, poorly sighted people in Britain today do not appear to be
materially worse off than others of a similar age; they have usually
lived for many years in the community that surrounds them (80 per

cent for more than 10 years) and are in as much, or as little, contact with caring services as other elderly people not characterised as having poor sight.[8] One in two are not in contact with any service. Fewer than half consider poor sight to be chief among their problems, and less than a third consider their lives in any way curtailed by it — most of those who do not have some other major difficulty to contend with.[8,16] Very few have had any specific technical help for their visual difficulties; even among those registered as 'blind', no more than 10 per cent can read Braille, and over three-quarters have no talking books, though both these are among the supposed 'benefits' of registration.[25] One in five live alone and a further half with a spouse or relative of similar age — the remaining 30 per cent live with a relative of a younger generation, usually a daughter.

However, in assessing the help that elderly people with poor sight may need, two further points need to be made. The first is that whether they are at home or in hospital,[8,16,26,27] as many as half of elderly people with visual disability have never had a specialist assessment of their eye problems, though most can be helped dramatically by quite simple means. There is support for these findings from the USA and elsewhere.[22,28] Whether such unreported needs are due to low expectations, acceptance of disability or denial, they often lead to unnecessary hardship and dependence. The second point is that where another major disability impinges on the life of an elderly poorly sighted person, usually an arthritic or circulatory problem, it is much more likely to be known to the medical services, and some sort of help provided for it.[13,14] It is poor vision (and hearing loss) that remains the Cinderella, unidentfied and forgotten.

## References

1. *National Assistance Act*(1948)
2. *Blind Person's Act*(1920)
3. Nizetic, B. (1975) 'Public Health Ophthalmology' in W. Hobson (ed.), *The Theory and Practice of Public Health*, Oxford University Press, London
4. Platt, P. (1950) 'Additional Factors Affecting the Blind' in P. Zahl (ed.), *Blindness*, Princeton University Press, Princeton, New Jersey
5. Kemp, N. J. (1981) *Current Psychological Reviews*, vol. 1, pp. 69–89
6. Ashcroft, S. C. (1963) 'Blind and Partially Sighted Children' in L. M. Dunn (ed.), *Exceptional Children in Schools*, Holt, Rinehart and Winston, New York
7. Luke, I. and Whiteman, M. (1972) *The Social Sources of Adjustment to Blindness*, American Foundation for the Blind, New York

8. Cullinan, T. R. (1977) 'The Epidemiology of Visual Disability. Studies of Visually Disabled People in the Community', *University of Kent, HSRU Report No. 28*

9. Hilbourne, J. (1973) 'On Disabling the Normal', *British Journal of Social Work*, December

10. DHSS (1979) 'Blindness and Partial Sight in England 1969–1976' *Reports on Public Health and Medical Subjects, No. 129*, DHSS, HMSO, London

11. Knight, R. and Warren, M. D. (1978) 'Physically Disabled People Living at Home. A Study of Numbers and Needs', *Reports on Health and Social Subjects, No. 13*, DHSS, HMSO, London

12. Siller, J. (1972) in: 'Science and Blindness. Retrospective and Prospective', *American Foundation for the Blind Inc.* New York

13. Fitzgerald, R. (1970) 'Reactions to Blindness: An Exploratory Study of Adults With Recent Loss of Sight', *Arch. of Clin. Psych. (1970)*, vol. 22, pp. 276–86

14. Keegan, D., Ash, D. and Greenough, T. (1975) 'Adjustment to Blindness', *Canad. J. Ophth.*, vol. 11, no. 22

15. Hicks, D. (1976) *Primary Health Care: A Review*, HMSO, London

16. Calnan, S. (1981) 'Elderly People with Poor Sight at Home', *Depart. of Preventive Medicine, St Bartholomew's Hosp. Med. Coll.*, M. Phil

17. Silver, J., Gould, E., Thomsitt, J. (1974) 'The Provision of Low Vision Aids to the Visually Handicapped', *Trans. Ophth. Soc. UK*, vol. XCIV, part 1

18. Lukoff, I. and Whiteman, M. (1963) 'Attitudes and Blindness: Components, Correlates and Effects', *Vocational Rehab. Admin. US Dept of HEW*

19. Kemp, N. J. (1981) 'Social Psychological Aspects of Blindness: A Review' *Current Psychological Reviews*, vol. 1, pp. 69–89

20. Delafield, G. (1976) 'Adjustments to Blindness', *New Outlook For the Blind*, February, pp. 64–8

21. Armstrong, D. (1981) 'Pathological Life and Death: Medical Specialization and Geriatrics', *Social Science and Medicine*, vol. 15A, pp. 253–7

22. Kornzweig, D. *et al.* (1975) 'The Eye in Old Age', *Am. J. of Ophthal.*, vol. 44, p. 29

23. Fenton, P. U. *et al.* (1975) 'Evaluation of Vision in Slow Stream Wards', *Age and Ageing* vol. 4, p. 43

24. Schon, D. (1972) 'Research on the Blindness Systems' in M. D. Graham (ed.), 'Science and Blindness', *American Foundation for the Blind*, New York

25. Gray, P. G. and Todd, J. (1965) 'Mobility and Reading Habits of The Blind', *Government Social Survey*, HMSO, London

26. Chamberlain, J. (1975) 'Validation of Screening Tests for Unreported Disability in the Elderly', Dept. of Comm. Med., University College Hospital, London

27. Williamson, J. (1964) 'Old People at Home — Their Unreported Needs', *Lancet*, May, vol. 1, pp. 1117–20

28. Josephson, E. And Sussman, M. B. (1962/1963) 'A Pilot Study of Visual Impairment', *American Foundation for the Blind*, New York

# 2 EPIDEMIOLOGY

## United Kingdom

While fairly up-to-date figures are available for the total of registered 'blind' people in Britain, and somewhat less so for those registered as 'partially sighted', it is much harder to estimate how many people in the community have a serious sight problem yet are not registered. In 1981 about 110,000 people in England were registered as blind; 230 for every 100,000 in the total population.[1] The figures for 'partial sight' were much smaller (largely for the reasons given in Chapter 1) — about 55,000, or 110 per 100,000 total population. But is has been estimated that the blind register underestimates by about 30 per cent[2] the number of people living at home who might be eligible for inclusion, and the partial sight register by about 50 per cent.[3]

In our modern and ageing society, the great preponderance of diseases leading to visual disability are related to old age, so it is not surprising to find that the age-specific prevalence rates for both blindness and partial sight for older people are much higher than the general ones above. Between the ages of 75–79 years, just over 1 per cent of people are registered as blind; over the age of 85 years, just over 5 per cent.[1] However, as has been indicated, it is also the elderly who do not become registered, so the true levels of those eligible are higher than this.

Every year some 12,500 people are added to the blind register in England and Wales, almost 85 per cent of whom are in their retirement years.[4] Somewhat fewer, about 10,000, become registered as partially sighted, but only 70 per cent are elderly. This undoubtedly reflects the lack of perceived (and·actual) benefits to becoming registered as partially sighted, but it also reflects the difference in the occurrence and progression of sight-threatening diseases at different ages (Chapter 4), as well perhaps, as the inclination of ophthalmic specialists to bring as many benefits as possible to old people in patent need.

A recent study commissioned by the Royal National Institute for the Blind (RN13) has made some interesting forecasts of how

numbers will look in 1991 and 2001.[1] Taking all factors into con-
sideration, including population numbers, age changes, the possible impact of new technology and allowing for under-registration
at its present rate, the suggestion is that the number of visually
disabled people aged 75 years or more who are eligible for registration as blind (in England) will increase from 84,500 at present
(estimated) to 98,000 in 1991, and then fall slightly to 97,300 in
2001. The study does not produce a similar age estimate for partial
sight.

While it is relatively easy to keep figures and produce analyses
of those who are registered, it is much harder to deduce estimates
of those who are not. However, attempts have been made; though
most of them, both local and national, have included vision as only
one among a number of handicapping conditions.

The first major survey, known as the 'Harris' survey, was in
1968/69[5] and included questions on 'blindness' in a national
random sample of some 245,000 households in Great Britain. The
survey concentrated on the difficulties in various aspects of work,
leisure and living experienced by people as a result of impairments
or handicaps. It did not attempt to ascribe single causes.
'Blindness' was loosely defined as a self-declared inability to see,
to read or write or to recognise a friend across the street — a far
wider and more subjective concept than that used for registration,
though it did include an element of near vision.

Subsequently, there have been many similar, though more local,
surveys, mostly in response to the exhortations of the Chronic
Sick and Disabled Persons Act (1970).[6] The Act enjoined local
authorities to discover how many disabled people lived in their
areas and might be in need of services; however, 'need' was to be
defined in terms of what was (locally) available and not in the
perceptions of the handicapped people themselves. Inevitably, the
efforts expended by the various authorities corresponded fairly
closely to their willingness to meet needs. Some approached all
households, some only a sample; some did no more than distribute
leaflets and some did nothing at all. Almost all those who did take
up the challenge modelled their surveys along the lines of the
'Harris' survey and relied on handicapped people to identify themselves, usually in response to a postal questionnaire. Only a few
validated their results by approaching a sample of households
where no such identifications had been made. The results of the
surveys, predictably variable, have been summarised by Knight

and Warren[7] who also describe the methods used. Their estimates of disability and handicap are in the same sort of range as the earlier ones of Harris,[5] but they also lay stress on the importance of such surveys in raising local awareness of handicap and what it means in an urgent, modern society.

Among the most comprehensive and best designed of the local authority studies was the Canterbury Survey of Handicapped People (1972).[8] It had the outstanding feature that it was repeated two years later to see what good had come to those identified as being in need in the first round. It also had a new and unique feature for those who claimed that they had 'difficulty in seeing to read and get about'. A simple sight test of near and distant vision was administered in each person's home by lay interviewers who had no more than basic training in the use of sight test cards and in how to obtain the best available light. With each person's permission, it was then possible to compare the results obtained at home with the results at a recent hospital clinic visit, where this had occurred, and to show that the two corresponded fairly accurately. A later study[9] showed that practically all the discrepancies between the two sets of measurements could be explained on the basis of poor home lighting; so, for the first time, it was demonstrated that sufficiently accurate estimates of visual acuity can be made by non-specialist observers in the homes of visually disabled people, almost all of whom were elderly, on which judgements about the need for further specialist help could be made.

The experience and many of the methods, including sight testing, of the Canterbury survey were used in a national survey of England and Wales (1977), which was designed to discover the needs of disabled and handicapped people principally in terms of the compensation and benefits they had received.[10] The survey added considerably to knowledge of the difficulties of visually disabled people and of the relative importance of the various diseases leading to it. It also confirmed the ease of using sight test cards at home and the considerable potential benefits in doing so.

Many other studies have been done on more limited groups of people; limited by membership of a particular general practice or group of practices, by ages sometimes rather arbitrarily chosen, or because they belong to some particular institution such as a school, hospital or the armed forces. Of the few studies that have been directed particularly towards elderly people living at home, it is surprising how many have imposed an upper age limit of 80 or 85 years for no obvious reason, except perhaps the supposed ease of obtaining information. This severely limits their general usefulness. Only a few studies have concerned themselves with elderly people in residential care; among the best of them is Fenton's (1975) study in geriatric wards in Portsmouth,[11] which showed that not only the prevalence of poor sight but the need for help is practically the same inside hospital as it is in the community at large.

It is possible to draw the following conclusions from the mass of data provided by these studies:

1. For every 100,000 adults of all ages living at home in England and Wales, about 520 are visually disabled according to WHO criteria. In an average health district of some 200,000 people (all ages), there are about 1,000 visually disabled people living at home. This figure will be nearer 1,200 if the population of the district is elderly.

2. A little over half of the visually disabled adults will be registered at any one time, and so known to the social services.

3. Seventy-five per cent (that is, about 750) of visually disabled adults will be in their retirement years and about half (500) over the age of 75. The greatest amount of unmet need arises among the elderly.

Figure 1 illustrates the best estimates available of the range of visual acuities (distance) among visually disabled adults living at home.[10] It can be seen that if the registration criteria for 'partial sight' are interpreted very liberally, some 60 per cent of visually disabled people, according to the WHO classification, might be eligible for registration but that a further 30 per cent, all of them with considerable sight difficulties, would still be excluded. It also suggests that at least one in 10 visually disabled people are so handicapped by other illnesses that they are not able to manage sight tests.

There are undoubted variations in the number of registered elderly people in different parts of the country that cannot be explained on the basis of age distribution and registration practices alone, although these certainly account for the greater part of the variation.[1] No studies have yet been done on ethnic minorities (some of whom have a predisposition to certain sight-threatening eye diseases, notably cataract and glaucoma) but, in the main, they have not yet been long enough in this country to provide an elderly population. No major 'blinding' disease has a disposition

## Figure 1: Percentage Distribution of Different Levels of Visual Acuity among Visually Disabled People Living at Home

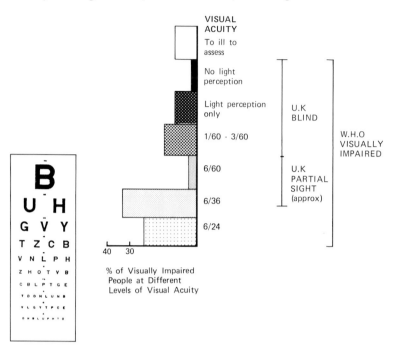

% of Visually Impaired
People at Different
Levels of Visual Acuity

Source: Cullinan (1977)[10]

towards one or other sex, so the presence in the population of far more elderly visually disabled women than men is no more than an expression of the differences that exist in the population as a whole.

Finally, a big national survey of handicapping conditions is planned by the office of Population Census and Surveys for 1985 and this will undoubtedly improve on the estimates provided here, as well as give more insights into the living conditions and difficulties of visually disabled elderly people living at home. Sight testing will be included for all those declaring a difficulty.

## Visual Disability Around the World

### Industrialised Societies

Nations, understandably, do not record figures about disabilities unless they have the social or economic ability to do something about them. Therefore, it is to the wealthier countries that we must look for the most accurate figures with which to compare Britain's; countries that also have, in the main, populations of approximately the same age structure as Britain's. Even so, the restrictions imposed by the many different definitions of 'blindness', both on the people they seek to serve and the data that accrue from them, are as apparent elsewhere as they are here; though in some countries, notably in the United States and Canada, the definitions are somewhat more liberal, and embrace Britain's concept of 'partial sight'.

Nowhere can someone identify himself as 'blind', 'partially sighted' or 'visually disabled' and automatically receive benefit as a result. Questions related to 'blindness' used to be asked in the census in Britain between 1851 and 1911, and until as late as 1940 in the United States. But they did not lead to any benefit for the individual and the inaccuracies were huge: compared to local surveys, the census returns consistently underestimated those who were truly 'blind', whatever the current legal definition of that word.[12] People, particularly elderly people, were extremely reluctant to identify themselves as 'blind' on such an impersonal document as a census return. In Canada, where the census question appeared until more recently, it was estimated that actual registration was double that of corresponding census returns.[13]

Few countries now depend entirely on census returns to estimate the prevalence of 'blindness': Kuwait, Portugal, Turkey, Greece, Gibralter and Japan are among them, though they do not regularly publish data.[14] Mauritius and St Helena — small islands where census counting is presumably much easier to verify — have produced more recent figures.

Few countries that keep, and publish, regular data based on 'blind registration' are in any doubt about their inconsistencies and inaccuracies and the reasons for them. Many have made periodic attempts to reach beyond legal definitions of 'blindness' and to find out the true extent of visual disability in the population. The most obvious way is to take a supposedly random sample of people and ask some simple question that is believed to indicate how well they can see. The United States' national interview surveys did just this in 1957–58, 1959–61 and 1963–65, using a 'representative' sample of 21,000 individuals on each occasion.[12] They were asked if they could 'read ordinary newsprint even with the aid of glasses': the resulting estimates of 'blindness', based solely on those who said they could not, were almost three times as high (570:100,000 total population) as those from registration (6/60 Snellen or less in the better eye has been accepted by most states since 1955). Although such an approach gets nearer to a concept of perceived visual disability than does the measurement of visual acuity, to use near vision in the question and distance vision to register is a clear disadvantage, and has never worked whenever it has been tried.[15]

An alternative method is to measure the vision of a sample of the population without asking any questions related to what can be seen. This was done during the 1960–62 National Health Examination Survey in the United States on a 'probability' sample of 6,672 people aged between 18 and 79 years. Very high estimates of legal 'blindness' resulted: eight out of every 1,000 (total population) with sight no better than 6/60 Snellen, even though people over 80 years of age were excluded. However, since 'usual' rather than 'best' lens correction was used, the statistic implies considerable doubt. A similar survey was undertaken in 1971–72, although the upper age limit was even lower, at 74 years.[16] The sample size was also more limited and, probably, to a degree self-selective but considerable care was paid to obtain accurate measurement of visual acuity. A more modest estimate of 'blindness', much nearer that derived from registration data of two per 1,000 total population, was derived.

Similar surveys have been reported from Northern Canada[17] where eye disease among the Eskimo population is particularly prevalent, and from Iceland where glaucoma in the elderly is a severe problem.[18] In this latter survey, figures as high as 3:1,000 total population with a visual acuity of 3/60 or less (approximately equivalent to blindness in England and Wales) were obtained with a similar population structure. This implies figures some 30 per cent higher than in England and Wales, but it is instructive that the actual proportion of those who were registered in Iceland was precisely the same as in England, despite the Icelandic definition of blindness being an inability 'to find (their) way in places unknown to them before, by means of (their) sight'.

Perhaps, though, the most revealing recent comparison between people prepared to identify themselves as visually disabled and those found during a survey comes from Egypt[19] where 2,970 per 100,000 people examined during a 4 per cent random population sample in Alexandria were found to have a visual acuity of 6/60 or less, compared to only 1,290 per 100,000 who came forward voluntarily for eye examination. These figures are, of course, enormously high by 'Western' standards, though the population structure of Egypt is somewhere between that of 'developing' and 'developed' countries. What is instructive, though, is that it was elderly men and women in both town and country as well as women in general who were under-represented among those declaring themselves to be in need.

But surveys are extremely expensive undertakings and can only be done occasionally, at least on a scale large enough to yield generally representative results. Most countries with registers have to rely on them for making plans and publishing data; and those without only do surveys when they can identify a section of the population in particular need, often economic or educational. Occasional attempts have been made to improve registration data: one such was the Model Reporting Area Scheme in the United States when several States agreed to abide by a strict protocol designed to improve both the completeness of registration and the epidemiological data derived from it. It did not last long, however — the effort proved too costly and was abandoned in 1971. This apart, little formal validation of registration exists anywhere and the disparites are much the same now as they always have been. Even between the different regions of a single country, they are often considerable.[20,21]

*Developing Countries*

Despite their generally much younger populations, the great majority of the world's 16,000,000 'blind' people live in countries poorly equipped economically either to prevent blindness or to cure it.

Figure 2 illustrates the huge differences in the prevalence of 'blindness' that exist between Western nations and the 'Third World'. The figure is based on whole-population survey and registration data published within the last 20 years.

Although a small part of the differences between countries can be explained on the basis of different definitions, ascertainment techniques and population age, by far the greater part is due to the

## Figure 2: Comparative Figures for Blindness (Selected Countries)

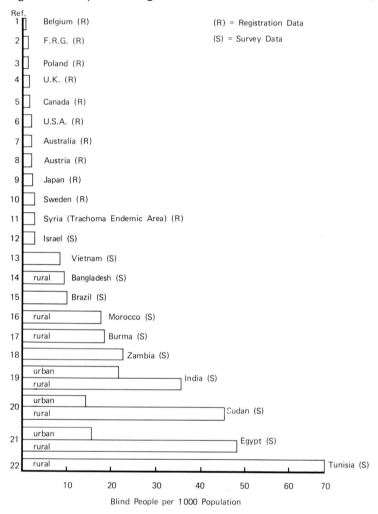

Source: WHO (1979)

**REFERENCES ( reproduced by permission of the World Health Organisation from WHO unpublished document)**

1. *Epidemiological and Vital Statistics Report* (1966), vol. 19; pp. 437–511
2. *Medizinische Klinik* (1968), vol. 68; pp. 279–82
3. WHO (1972), Document A 25/10
4. WHO Unpublished Data (1980)
5. PAKO/WHO (1979) Document DPC/PBL/1.0/79

6. Ibid
7. WHO Unpublished Data (1978)
8. WHO (1972), Document A 25/10
9. World Council For The Welfare Of The Blind (1976), The Asian Blind No P
10. WHO Unpublished Data (1978)
11. International Congress For Prevention Of Blindness (1974), Cairo, pp. 19–20
12. Epidemiological And Vital Statistics Report (1966), vol. 19; pp. 439–511
13. WHO (1981), Document WPR/PBL/INF.81.12
14. *Bangladesh Medical Research Council Bulletin* (1976), vol. 2; 71–4.
15. WHO Unpublished Data (1973)
16. WHO (1979), MOR/PPS/001
17. *Bull. World Health Organization* (1978), vol. 56; pp. 945–55
18. WHO Unpublished Data (1978)
19. *J. Of The Indian Med. Assoc.* (1976), vol. 67; p. 234.
20. *Bull. Of Ophthal. Soc. Of Egypt* (1976), vol. 69; pp. 629–33
21. *Int. Congress For Prev. Of Blindness* (1974), Cairo; pp. 19–20
22. *Brit. J. Ophthal* (1976), vol. 60; pp.245–52

presence of one or more specific blinding diseases with minimal facilities in prevention or treatment. Where these diseases are most prevalent (trachoma, for instance, in North Africa and cataract in India), the differences between rural and urban populations tend to be very great — so much so that many poor countries have directed such surveys as they have been able to afford mainly to the villages where they know the problem to be worst.

Since in most of these countries about 80 per cent of the population lives in the rural areas and is wholly dependent on agriculture for a livelihood, with no sort of formalised disability relief, the economic effect of blinding diseases is enormous. In general, the diseases develop very much earlier in life than do the sight-threatening diseases of the West, often attacking in childhood (xerophthalmia, trachoma), young adult life (onchocerciasis, trachoma) or during those years when families are dependent on the breadwinner (cataracts, glaucoma, injuries). Since none of these are life-threatening diseases, there will be a considerable increase in the number of people facing a disabled old age as the populations of these countries get older.

It will take a sustained effort in public health and curative medicine to halt, let alone reverse, this situation, though undoubtedly huge strides have recently been made at least in the fields of trachoma, xerophthalmia and onchocerciasis.

Despite the manifest difficulties in comparing figures, there are some intriguing differences exhibited in Figure 2 even between countries that, superfically, might be supposed to have much the same sort of climatic and other problems. Sixteen per cent of adult 'blindness' in Bangladesh, for instance, is ascribed to glaucoma, while it makes up less than 0.5 per cent in India; in North Africa, trachoma seems to have a much more devastating effect than in Burma or Vietnam, where it is also the commonest ascribed cause of 'blindness'. But even within the elderly populations of Europe, there are also significant differences: in each country, about 20 per cent of those registered are in their retirement years, yet senile cataract seems to be far more common in Austria than in, say, Belgium.

There is a great need for better population studies of specific diseases both among the younger population of the developing world and the older ones of the West, but such studies must be based on strict diagnostic criteria and sound epidemiological principles. Neither population surveys nor registration practices can do more than point to possible areas of interest.

**References**

1. Initial Demographic Study (1984) *Report for the Royal National Institute for the Blind, June 1984*, Shankland Cox, London
2. Graham, P., Wallace, J., Welsby, E. and Grace, H. (1968) 'Evaluation of Postal Detection of Registerable Blindness', *British Journal of Preventive and Social Medicine*, vol. 22, p. 238
3. Page, J. (1974) 'Definition of Blindness and Partial Sight', in M. D. Graham (ed.), *Technological Prosthetics for the Partially Sighted*, IIASA
4. DHSS (1979) 'Blindness and Partial Sight in England 1969–1976', *Reports on Public Health and Medical Subjects, No. 129*, DHSS, HMSO
5. Harris, A. *et al.* (1971) *Handicapped and Impaired in Great Britain*, OPCS
6. *Chronically Sick and Disabled Person's Act 1970*, HMSO, London
7. Knight, R. and Warren M. D. (1978) 'Physically Disabled People Living at Home. A Study of Numbers and Needs', *Reports on Health and Social Subjects, No. 13*, DHSS, HMSO, London
8. Warren, M. D. (1974) The Canterbury Survey of Handicapped People, *University of Kent, HSRU Report No. 6*
9. Cullinan, T., Silver, J., Gould, E. and Irvine, D. (1979) 'Visual Disability and Home Lighting', *Lancet*, vol. I, p. 642–4
10. Cullinan, T. R. (1977) 'The Epidemiology of Visual Disability. Studies of Visually Disabled People in the Community', *University of Kent, HSRU Report No. 28*
11. Fenton, P., Arnold, R. and Wilkins, P. (1975) 'Evaluation of Vision in Slow Stream Wards', *Age and Ageing*, vol. 4, p. 43
12. Goldstein, H. (1972) *Demography of Blindness* in *'Science and Blindness'*, American Foundation for the Blind, New York
13. MacDonald, A. (1965) Causes of Blindness in Canada, *Canadian Medical Association Journal*, vol. 92, pp. 264–78
14. WHO (1966) 'Blindness Information Collected from Various Sources', *Epidem. Vital Statistics Report*, vol. 19, pp. 437–511
15. Josephson, E. and Sussman, M. B. (undated) 'A Pilot Study of Visual Impairment (1962/1963)', *American Foundation for the Blind*

16. 'Monocular Visual Acuity of Persons 4–74 years (1971–72)', *US Dept. of MEW Series*, vol. 11, no. 201
17 .Wyatt, H. T. (1973) 'Abnormalities of Cornea Lens and Retina: Survey Findings', *Artic Ophthal. Symposium, Can J. of Ophthal.*, April, vol 8
18. Bjornsson, G. (1955) 'Prevalence and Causes of Blindness in Iceland', *Am. J. of Ophthal.* vol. 39, pp. 202–8
19. Said, M. E., Goldstein, H., Korra, A., El-Kashlan, K. (1972) 'Blindness Prevalence Rates in Egypt', *HSMHA Reports*, vol. 87, no. 2
20. Brennan, M. E. and Knox, F. G. (1973) 'An Investigation into the Purpose, Accuracy and Effective Use of the Blind Register in England', *Brit. J. Prev. and Social Med.* vol. 27, pp. 154–9
21. Graham, P. A., Wallace, J., Welsby, E. and Grace H. J. (1968) 'Evaluation of Postal Detection of Registrable Blindness', *Brit. J. Prev. and Soc. Medicine*, vol. 22, p. 238

# 3 THE EYE AND HOW IT AGES

The eye is often compared to a camera. It does, of course share many of the optical principles of a modern camera but it is a far more sophisticated instrument than any manufacturer has dreamed up yet. It can do two things that no camera, however refined, can do; it can repair itself, to an extent at least, when it is damaged and it can alter the focal length of one of its refracting mechanisms, the lens, by changing its shape. On the other hand, it is subject to the same ageing process as all living tissue. In trying to understand some of the difficulties of elderly people with poor sight, it is useful to examine how each of the main components of the optical system changes with advancing years.

Figure 3: Diagram of the Eye. (For diagrammatic simplicity the macula has been drawn above the optic nerve. In fact it lies to one side)

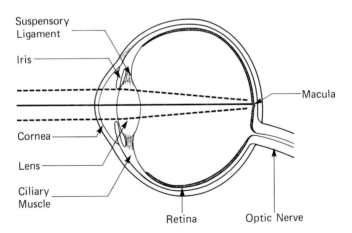

First, though, a brief reminder of how the eye works. Figure 3 illustrates the simple optical principles involved in producing an image on the sensitive retina that the brain can interpret, with experience, as a representation of the world outside. The objective

26

is, of course, to get the image of an object into focus on the retina however far away or near it is. This is done by using the refractive properties of the various substances through which the light rays pass from the object looked at. The light rays may originate from the object itself, as in looking at a candle flame or light bulb, or more often, they may be reflected from a source elsewhere.

Whenever light passes from one translucent medium to another (solid, liquid or gas) the rays may be refracted (deflected): the extent to which this occurs depends on the angle at which they hit the surface of the medium they are entering and on the refractive power, or index, of the medium. If they pass straight through, meeting the surface at right angles, then they are not refracted at all. The main refracting elements in the eye are the cornea and the lens (Figure 3) — the cornea retains its shape however much focusing is to be done; the lens is capable of altering its curvature ('accommodating') so that the image of the object is finally brought to the retina as clearly as possible.

The shape of the lens is determined by the action of the ciliary muscle which encloses it and to which it is attached by suspensory ligaments (Figure 3). When near objects are to be seen clearly, the ciliary muscles of each eye contract, slackening the suspensory ligaments and allowing the lens to become more rounded, principally on its outward, or anterior, surface. When the muscles are at rest and the ligaments tense, this surface is flatter than the inner or posterior surface. The effect of accommodation is to shorten the focal length of the lens, thus allowing for the fact that the rays of light from the near object to be seen strike the eye (the cornea) at a much sharper angle than if it were far away, and so would otherwise produce a sharp image 'behind' the retina.

It is one of the properties of lenses, and of curved translucent surfaces like the cornea, that the more powerful they are the more distorted are the rays that pass through them as these rays become progressively further from the central axis (spherical aberration). To limit this distortion, when the lens accommodates to focus on a near object, the iris (see Figure 3) tends to constrict to narrow the size of the pupil and so allow through only those rays of light nearer the centre of the lens — it is possible to focus accurately on a small, near object but not on a large one.

At the same time, both eyes are directed so that the centre of the image falls on the most sensitive part of the retina, the macula. This is done by the contraction, and corresponding relaxation, of the muscles outside the eyeball which govern its position in its socket. The cornea, of course, also acts as a major refracting surface and possesses the same tendency to distort those parts of a picture that fall furthest from its central axis. In partial compensation for this spherical aberration, neither the cornea nor the lens are in fact segments of true spheres, but tend to flatten out peripherally.

The 'depth' of focus of the young eye is considerable — everything more than six metres away is in focus on the retina when the lens is 'at rest', though clearly the resolution of detail is not very great. Nearer to six metres, the young eye begins to accommodate by progressively thickening its lens until, with considerable muscular effort, it can still see sharply objects only a few centimetres away. Its ability to determine details is considerable: it can, given good conditions of light, colour and contrast, distinguish between points of only two tenths of a millimetre apart, though even closer can be managed between two lines, presumably because more retinal cells are involved. The importance of being able to bring small objects, and at least the most interesting details of larger objects, into sharp focus on the most sensitive part of the retina — and being able to do it with both eyes at once — can hardly be overstated, especially in a modern world where near objects have the greatest impact on our daily lives. The total 'refractive' power of the human eye is about 60 dioptres — of which the cornea contributes about 44 dioptres and the lens the remaining 16 — when it is at its most accommodated.[1] (A dioptre is a measure of the refracting power of a lens or of a rounded surface acting as a lens; it is the reciprocal of the focal length measured in metres. Thus a lens with a focal length of two metres has a dioptre power of 1/2.)

It is apparent, then, that to achieve a clear image on the macula, a sharply defined object must be seen in a good light by an eye with its powers of accommodation intact (or with adequate lens correction), and with the various structures which transmit the light being healthy, unimpeded and transparent. The macula and the surrounding retina must also be intact, healthy and unobstructed for the image to be accurately interpreted, and the nerve connections to a healthy brain must be unimpeded. All these components of a good optical system are involved to a greater or lesser degree in the process of ageing or in the environment in which elderly people live, and many of them are considerably worsened by disease. The remainder of this chapter will outline briefly the effects of ageing on the human eye; Chapter 4 will deal with the common diseases that limit sight in old age and Chapter 7 will examine the effects of the environment on vision.

## The Ageing Eye

Weale has made a comprehensive study of the structural and functional changes that occur in the various components of the eye as it gets progressively older.[1,2] Much of what follows is taken from his excellent work, and concerns the later years of life alone.

### The Cornea

As age progresses the cornea becomes gradually more opaque so that more light must pass through it to produce the same intensity of image on the retina of the old eye as in the young one — this occurs especially in the ultraviolet end of the range. At the same time, possibly due to the depositing of fat (cholesterol) among the bundles of fibres that make up its structure, light passing through the cornea tends to be more scattered in old age, so marring the clarity of the image. However, it does not seem to be until the age of 70 or so that this becomes a difficulty, and, in the main, significant clouding or distortion of the cornea is usually due to disease rather than a simple ageing process.

### The Lens

The less contributes more than any other part of the eye to the visual consequences of the ageing process; it becomes thicker, stiffer and denser — all as a result of biochemical changes both in its nucleus and its capsule. It also moves forward in the eyeball. The net effect — and it is a 'net' effect, being far more complex than has sometimes been supposed — is to reduce the accommodating power of the lens so that it becomes progressively less able to shorten its focal length and thus produce on the retina a sharp image of near objects.

Most people begin to notice this effect (presbyopia) in their 40s as they find it harder and harder to read or do close work, but the process has been going on slowly since, at least, the end of adolescence. The eye does have some compensating mechanisms: the pupil, for instance, tends to be narrower, thus restricting light rays to the most effective part of the lens. There is some benefit, too, to those who have been mildly myopic (short-sighted) in earlier life. Since they have an eyeball longer than is normal, they have needed concave lenses to bend light rays from distant objects outwards before they reach the cornea, so that an image can be brought sharply on to the retina through a resting lens with a focal length too short for the eyeball. Now, with a lens less inclined to accommodate, they can sometimes discard their glasses and read in comfort. Presbyopia tends to be progressive through the 50s and 60s, though the rate of progression varies greatly in different people. Progression seems to slow down considerably after that. It is, of course, almost always possible to correct with adequate convex lenses.

## Ciliary Body

The tissue that surrounds the lens and in which the ciliary muscle lies changes considerably as age progresses, becoming generally thicker. This is important because the pressure inside the eyeball, which keeps the retina from crumpling, is maintained by a watery fluid (aqueous fluid) continuously put out by the ciliary body and draining away into the main bloodstream by way of minute pores between the iris and the cornea (the trabeculae). They lie at the bottom of a narrow circular drain (the angle of the anterior chamber) which, with the thickening of the lens and of the ciliary body, tends to get narrower and narrower with age. Normally, this does not matter but occasionally the drain blocks altogether — often when the ciliary muscle is relaxed and the pupil dilated. The fluid, being unable to escape, accumulates to give a sudden rise in pressure inside the eyeball (closed-angle glaucoma).

## The Retina

While the most sensitive part of the retina, the macula, is excellent at fine discrimination, it is to the remainder of the retina that a wide visual field and vision in conditions of near darkness are due. The macula is capable of fine colour distinction only when the light is good. The cone cells in the macula are also responsible for the high resolution of fine details and contrasts. The retina is richly supplied with blood vessels and many of the functional changes in the retina that occur with age can be ascribed to changes in its vascular bed. As elsewhere in the body, the vessels narrow and become more pervious and this affects the integrity of the highly sensitive retinal cells, as well as their ability to regenerate.[2]

But there are other effects of ageing too: fats and fibrous strands are deposited among the cells and it may be that a lifetime of light bombardment also has a degenerative effect on the retinal cells. Studies of the function of the retina in old age are not numerous; they mostly depend on evoked light stimuli or on subjective responses to various thresholds of light, colour and contrast. One of the major difficulties is that the yellowing lens filters off blue/violet light and the relatively constricted pupil of later years cuts it down considerably so that comparing intensities on the retina with those in young eyes may be a difficult thing to achieve. It has not yet been resolved which of the various ageing processes, in so far as they are independent, has the greatest effect on function.[2]

In sum, though, it can be said that, with age, the macula loses some of its abilities in spatial discrimination and in black and white contrast as well as in flicker sensitivity, which is presumably of less importance in the day-to-day lives of elderly people. More important, though, are the changes in colour perception, which is chiefly diminished in the blue/violet wavelengths. Weale[2] reminds us of the diamond trades' complaints about the older stone sorters being less reliable than the young ones in distinguishing white from yellow diamonds: 'Even though they may be working in rooms facing north so as to obtain the maximum benefit from blue (high colour temperature) North light, their blue-absorbing lenses defeat this cunning device.' It may be, too, that the tendency of some old ladies to 'go mauve' is not seen by them as quite so remarkable as it is to their grandchildren.

## The Optic Nerve and the Brain

The optic nerve thickens a little with age, shows signs of degenerating and loses some of its fibres (axons).[3] The result is to slow conduction and reduce the number as well as the speed of messages reaching the brain. Many of the changes in the brain itself, which occur in that part of the cortex related to vision, as elsewhere,[2] can be related to changes in blood supply. The net effect is a considerable loss of functioning cells which must decrease the brain's abilities in discrimination of light stimuli, both in space and frequency.

But sorting out these effects from those principally due to retinal and other eye changes is not easy; in the absence of actual disease, it must be only exceptionally that the ageing process in the optic nerve pathways and the brain play a larger part in the loss of vision than do changes in the eye itself.

## Conclusion

In later life, then, the eye is obviously less efficient than the younger eye at many of the tasks that elderly people enjoy. It loses some of its ability to resolve details, to distinguish colours and contrasts and, of course, to focus — though this loss can largely be corrected optically. But it also transmits light far less effectively — Weale[1] has estimated that the total effect of the slightly dimmed cornea, a constricted pupil and a considerably denser lens is to deprive a tired retina of two-thirds of the light that a young retina receives. It is obvious that many of these difficulties must be mitigated if the vision of elderly people is to be improved.

## References

1. Weale, R. A. (1963) *The Ageing Eye*, H. K. Lewis & Co., London
2. — (1982) *A Biography of the Eye, Development, Growth, Age*, H. K. Lewis & Co., London
3. Vrabec, F. (1977) 'Age Changes of the Human Optic Nerve Head', *Albrecht von Graefes Arch. Klin. Exp. Ophthal.*, vol. 202, pp. 231–6

# 4 EYE DISEASES THAT LIMIT SIGHT IN LATER LIFE

In considering the common eye diseases that may diminish the sight of elderly people, three things are important to remember. The first is that the great majority of visually disabled older people enter their retirement years with 'normal' sight — or, at least, with no more than the presbyopia common to most people over the age of 45 years or so, coupled perhaps with the astigmatism, 'long' or 'short' sight, they have known all their years. Although the first signs of the diseases that later compromise vision may be apparent in middle age,[1,2] they usually pass unnoticed and it may be years before they give rise to any disability.

The second point is that almost all the major diseases are progressive and, untreated or unarrested, they are likely to cause gradually worsening sight, although this may be slow and by no means steady. Third, all elderly people with a visual disability in the WHO range (see Figure 1, Chapter 2) do actually have an eye disease (or a disease of the nervous system); they are not merely suffering from 'old eyes' or 'tired sight'.

These three points go some way towards explaining why so many elderly people accept poor sight as one of the inevitable penalities of old age. To an extent it is (Chapter 3), but eye disease has often to be actively sought because there is no dividing line in terms of vision between the natural ageing process of the eye and the malevolent effects of disease on that process, and because both may be amenable to much help. Cullinan[2] has shown that if elderly visually disabled people are asked what are their main difficulties in life, almost a half will not mention poor sight because they are so overwhelmed by some other handicapping disease. Yet to improve sight may be to make other handicaps much easier to bear.[3] In addition, it cannot be assumed that the regular visits to the optician during the middle years, which fall off so dramatically in old age,[2] provide a good way of detecting the diseases which will compromise sight in later life.

What then are the common eye diseases of old age and how may they be recognised? Figure 4 illustrates the approximate percentage frequency of various ascribed causes of visual disability

## Figure 4: The Chief Causes of Visual Disability among Visually Disabled People Living at Home

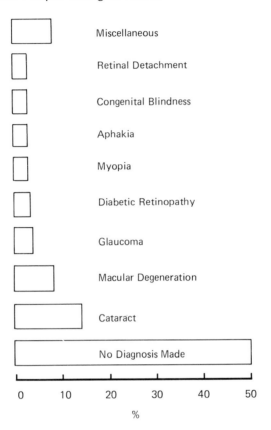

Source: Cullinan 1977[2]

among the 1,000 or so visually disabled adults in each health district of about 200,000 people. The figures are only approximate because hardly more than 50 per cent of elderly, visually disabled people have ever had a definite diagnosis made,[2] and because they are based on a fairly small (though nationally representative) sample. Diagnoses, too (even specialist ones), may vary quite a lot between observers.[4] Cataract heads the list of disease — but the presence of a dense central cataract may obscure a view of the retina, and retinal disease thus be missed. Macular degeneration is second, followed by glaucoma, and then, together, diabetic retinopathy, myopic atrophy and congenital blindness, each of which is likely to affect sight at a relatively younger age. Other causes, operative in old age, are retinal detachment and 'aphakia' — the loss of a lens, usually following extraction for cataract.

## Figure 5: Prevalence of Eye Disease in Middle-aged and Elderly People

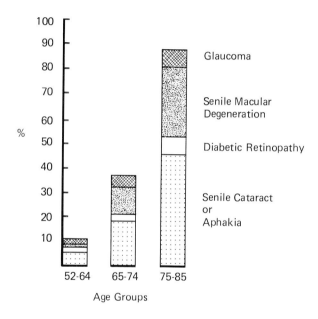

Source: Ederer (1977/78)[1], Framingham 1973–75

A slightly different perspective is presented by the Framingham Eye Study (Figure 5), a truly population-based study of eye disease in which all subjects were examined whether or not they identified a difficulty with sight. However, people over the age of 85 years were excluded and, for the important diseases of cataract and macular degeneration, only data from those whose sight was not absolutely normal (that is, was 6/9 or less) were analysed. There were certain weaknesses, too, in the final sample, but the results analysed by age group in Figure 5 give a

Figure 6: Chief Causes of Blind Registration in Later Life
(England and Wales)

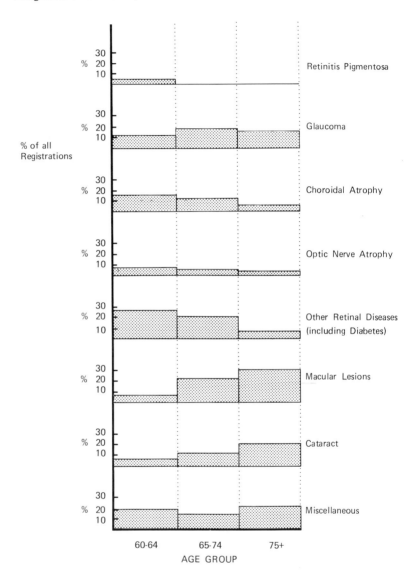

Source: Sorsby (1972) *The Incidence and Causes of Blindness in England and Wales, 1963–68* HMSO, London

good approximation of the prevalence of sight-threatening eye diseases in later life. They suggest that in the age group 75 to 85 years, almost nine out of 10 people have a diagnosable eye disease and that seven out of 10 have either a cataract or macular degeneration, or both. Despite this, 90 per cent of those with cataract were not visually disabled by WHO standards.[5] Finally, Figure 6 illustrates the diseases, at different ages, leading to registration as 'blind' in England in recent years. As years go by, macular degeneration becomes the most important cause. Taking Figures 5 and 6 in conjunction, it does seem that, in relation to its distribution in the general population, macular degeneration more often leads to *severe* sight loss in old people than any other disease and, pathologically, this is undoubtedly the case.

## Cataract

As Dobree points out,[6] the cataract that occurs in the elderly eye — unfortunately named 'senile cataract' — should no more be regarded as a disease than the whitening of hair. It is common, eventually, to everyone; if everyone lived to be 103, then all would have cataracts, though most people would not know it. A cataract, for the purposes of general understanding, can be taken as any opacity occurring anywhere in the lens — in its nucleus or inner part, which is the oldest part of the lens and is laid down in early intrauterine life, or in its outer layers in front of, round, or behind the nucleus (Figure 7). These layers are successively added throughout life, much like onion skins.

Once a cataract has formed it is not necessarily steadily progressive, but may remain small and untroublesome for years. Cataracts may be associated with external factors such as long exposure to ultraviolet light; they may be the result of intrauterine infection, most notably rubella (German measles); they may be associated with congenital abnormalities such as Down's syndrome. They may also occur after taking certain drugs for a long peiod — notably steroids, which are often used in the treatment of some arthritic conditions. But, undoubtedly, most cataracts, certainly those found in old age, are not associated with any of these known 'risk' factors. It is assumed that they are the consequence of the diminishing oxygen supply which accompanies the vascular changes of advancing years.

## Figure 7: Different Types of Lens Opacities

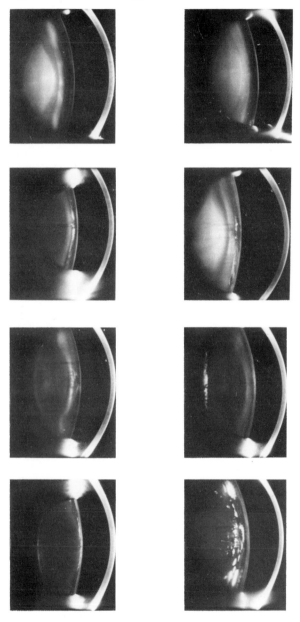

Source: Reproduced by kind permission of Professor O. Hockwin (Bonn)

Figure 8: Normal Vision

Figure 9: Cataract

*Symptoms*

The symptoms are entirely visual, though it must be remembered that most cataracts in elderly people cause no
symptoms at all. They depend not only on the density of the
cataract and its size, but in what part of the lens it lies. In
general, objects become increasingly more blurred and colours
more dull (Figures 8 and 9).

It may also be harder to read news print and, as Dobree says,[6]
the house may seem always to need redecorating. If the cataract
occupies the nucleus of the lens (Figure 7), the problems may be
equal whatever the light and no particular differences are noted
between outdoors and indoors. However, if the cataract is in the
front layers of the lens, (Figure 7) then 'glare' may be a particular
problem and the elderly person will express a preference for
subdued lighting. Those with cataracts chiefly in the back of the
lens (Figure 7) may be able to see distant objects clearly, but find
difficulty in reading and near vision because the cataract
coincides with the focal point of the lens when it is fully accommodated. However, a cataract confined to this part of the lens is
not common.

## Macular Degeneration

The macula, being the most sensitive part of the retina and
concerned primarily with fine discrimination and colour distinction, can be expected to declare quite easily when it stops
functioning well. It is a matter of some doubt whether the
changes seen in the degenerative macular diseases of old age are
different in kind from the normal ageing process or merely more
rapid and florid extensions of it.

The earliest changes that can be seen through the
ophthalmoscope are drusen — small, fluffy or discrete deposits
that appear under the floor of the macular area, deep to the
retinal pigment epithelium.[7] They are probably deposits pushed
out by ageing pigment cells, and they may be hard or soft (in
which case they tend to run together and be more rapidly
progressive). Drusen can be present for many years without
harming vision and a few 'hard' drusen at the macula can be
regarded as normal for old age.

It is when they enlarge, take on a softer, smudgier appearance, and begin to lose their soft edges that they seem to betoken more serious changes in the retina. When this happens, a layer of debris is laid down beneath the membrane on which the retinal pigment cells rest and they are lifted up from their bed and from their blood supply, and so lose their function. The blood vessels, too, may leak or even bleed — it is probably their slow degeneration that has contributed to the whole process anyway. In response to all this, new, weak and inadequate blood vessels may grow.

The appearances of macular degeneration vary according to how much lifting up of the sensitive layer of cells has occurred, how much debris has been deposited and how much bleeding or discharge from the vessels there has been. In general, two types of macular degeneration are described; a 'disciform' type which has large components of deposited material, and a 'vascular' type which is the result of much leakage or haemorrhage. Most degenerations are mixed, however, and the final results are much the same, though a proliferation of new vessels may predispose to more rapid progression.[8] In clinically obvious macular degeneration, the most easily seen changes through the ophthalmoscope are clumping of the retinal pigment cells and whitened areas of atrophy where cells have degenerated. But the area of damage seen with the ophthalmoscope is always less than the area of functional damage.[9]

*Symptoms*

The earliest symptom is often an increasing difficulty in distinguishing small objects and in doing fine tasks but, because the other eye comes to the rescue, this may pass unnoticed until either it too begins to deteriorate or the fine object in the most affected eye disappears altogether. Dobree gives a good stage-by-stage description over five years,[6] in which the first symptom noticed is a distortion of straight lines in the central vision of one eye so that shelves and picture rails appear to be kinked. This becomes considerably worse over two years or so; central vision in the first- affected eye becomes blurred and the other eye begins to manifest the same early distortions. Fine seeing has to be given up a year later, but large print can still be read.

Figure 10 is also illustrative because it shows the considerable image distortion round the 'lost' area of the macular. Even an

Figure 10: Macular Degeneration — View of Object in Figure 8

elderly person with such a disability may well retain considerable mobility, using peripheral vision, but she may be quite lost when it comes to fixating on a price label or recognising the faces of friends. So it is often the near vision tasks, those most dear to the elderly, which become impossible. Moreover, if signs of macular degeneration are present in one eye, they are normally present in the other, too. It is estimated that 10 to 15 per cent of people who have no macular function in one eye will lose the macular function of the other and that 60 to 70 per cent of people with macular degeneration will be reduced to 'registerable blindness' within five years of the onset of visual disability.[9]

## Diabetic Retinopathy

Although this condition is much less common as a cause of visual disability in the elderly than cataract or macular degeneration, it is likely to cause sight loss at an earlier age and is the commonest cause of new sight loss in middle age. There are two main types of diabetic retinopathy, though both can be present at the same time. The first, proliferative retinopathy, is more often associated with younger diabetic patients dependent on insulin.[10] There is a progressive growth of weak new vessels from the retinal arteries and veins which grow forward on the vitreous (inner) surface of the retina and are liable to rupture. Usually, this takes place slowly and in small amounts so that there is time for the clot to become organised and absorbed; but considerable bleeding into the vitreous may occur causing rapid sight loss if the rupture is sudden and fairly extensive.

More common among elderly people is the simple background type of diabetic retinopathy[10] associated with late-onset diabetes not dependent on insulin for its control. The essential lesion is a weakness of the small capillary blood vessels of the retina, commonly close to the macula, which bulge and form 'micro-aneurysims' observed as minute red dots through the ophthalmoscope. These sometimes leak, giving small haemorrhages and collections of plasma, so that the retina becomes oedematous. Over time, fats in the escaped plasma become deposited round the damaged capillaries and appear as white 'exudates'. There is not the risk of a sudden bleed as there is in the proliferative variety.

Figure 11: Diabetic Retinopathy — View of Object in Figure 8

*Symptoms*

Clearly symptoms depend on where on the retina the major manifestations of the disease are. The patient will notice an early deterioration of vision even in the absence of haemorrhage if either the proliferative or the exudative type affects the macula; but quite extensive patchy field loss can occur if most of the lesions are in the peripheral retina before it comes to the notice of an elderly person (Figure 11). But the serious sight implications of the background, exudative type are not to be under-rated; almost 40 per cent of elderly people in whom background retinopathy is discovered may suffer moderate or severe sight loss within five years of diagnosis. Finally, there is plausible evidence that the onset and the progress of retinopathy in younger adult life and childhood is related to disease control,[10] but how much this applies to the elderly remains uncertain.

## Glaucoma

Glaucoma occurs when the pressure inside the eyeball rises above normal and begins to affect the blood supply to the retina and optic nerve; it is almost always caused by a failure of the fluid inside the eye to drain adequately. There are two main types of primary glaucoma — closed-angle glaucoma and the more insidious open-angle type. The angle referred to is the gutter between the front surface of the iris and the transparent cornea (see Figure 3). The intraocular fluid drains from this gutter through a filter (the trabeculum) and so into the main blood circulation; the pores in the trabeculum, being very small, allow the fluid to drain only slowly, thus keeping up pressure inside the eyeball. Any obstruction to the flow causes the pressure to rise — suddenly if obstruction is sudden, but much more often slowly and insidiously.

The commonest form of glaucoma is the open-angle type in which the angle remains open but the pores of the trabeculum become gradually inadequate to filter the fluid fast enough. This usually happens, without symptoms, over many years until the intraocular pressure has risen above its normal value of 12 to 24mmHg to reach levels often above 30mm. This results in a gradually increasing bulging of the optic nerve head (the weakest part of the wall of the eyeball), which eventually compromises its blood supply and leads to death of the nerve fibres. The nerve head looks unduly white and 'cupped' through the ophthalmoscope.

About 1.5 per cent of all adults have raised intraocular pressure and the signs of 'glaucoma' around the nerve head. But there is a third element to the 'triad' usually needed for definitive diagnosis — the loss of visual field that results from nerve loss to the retina. This often starts above the macula and may pass unnoticed by the patient for a considerable time because it is only partial and at first affects only one eye (though the actual signs of glaucoma can usually be seen in both). Indeed, it is not until the macula is affected that many elderly people, used to near-vision tasks, may complain of difficulties with sight.

Closed or narrow-angle glaucoma is less common. Here, it is the gutter itself that becomes blocked, usually because a gradually thickening lens has pushed the iris into an unusually narrow gutter. Anything that now dilates the pupil (for example darkness or anger) may obliterate the angle altogether so that the outflow of intraocular fluid is blocked and pressure immediately begins to rise. However, the process is potentially reversible; with relaxation and better light, things can return to their precarious 'normal'. During the period of high pressure all that may be noticed is a mild discomfort, some mistiness of vision and a distortion of colours. This recurrent type of sub-acute closed- angle glaucoma is much commoner in some tropical countries, such as India, than it is in Western countries; and it is considerably more common among people from the West Indies, especially women.[11]

An acute congestive glaucoma results if the situation does not quickly resolve that may well lead to blindness. The intraocular pressure continues to rise, sometimes to as high as 60mmHg, and intense eye pain or severe headache is experienced, often with vomiting. It builds up over a few hours and is accompanied by increasing visual disturbance. At first a haziness, but later complete blindness, occurs in that eye. The eye looks red and congested and the pupil widely dilated. This is a medical emergency and urgent treatment is needed if sight is to be saved, because pressure inside the eye may well have risen above the point where blood can be pumped through the sensitive retina by the arteries supplying it. And, as Dobree puts it,[6] '. . . to make matters worse, the pain and anxiety of the attack often start off an acute attack in the second eye'.

Apart from these two distinct types of 'primary' glaucoma, closure of the angle can sometimes result from diseases in the structures round it ('secondary glaucoma'). Inflammation of the iris (iritis), tumours, or bleeding into the anterior chamber blocking the pores of the trabeculum are examples of this.

## Problems Round the Eye

Several problems affecting the eyelids and other structures round the eye are particularly common among the elderly; they are not serious, in general, but can cause great discomfort and occasionally loss of vision, either directly or as a result of their secondary efects.

## Herpes Zoster (shingles)

Herpes zoster (from the Greek, literally, a 'creeping belt') or 'shingles' (from the Latin, *cingere* to gird or encircle) occurs far more often in adults than in children, and reaches a peak of incidence in the seventies and early eighties. It commonly affects the trunk or upper abdomen, but shingles around the eye (herpes ophthalmicus) is also frequent in elderly people.

It is generally supposed that herpes zoster is caused by a reactivation of chicken pox virus which has lain dormant in deeply buried nerve cells for very many years. As a result of some stimulus, as yet unknown, the virus becomes active again and migrates along the whole length of the nerve until it reaches the surface and gives rise to the typical rash, indistinguishable from chicken pox, except for its more limited area.

Herpes has sometimes been observed to follow an injury or a debilitating ilness but if these are indeed predisposing factors they are not to be found in the great majority of people who acquire the disease. However, it is associated with the taking of drugs such as steroids and, possibly, antihistamines, and is one of the well-recognised hazards of the immunosuppressive regimes used in the treatment of certain kidney conditions and cancers.

Beliefs about the contagious nature of shingles are often in-accurate. It is rare for an adult to contract the disease after exposure to a child with chicken pox or another adult with shingles, if only because the supposed latent period of the disease is so long. It is easier for a child to contract chicken pox after exposure to herpes but far less easy than after exposure to chicken pox, where droplet infection plays so large a role. In practical terms, therefore, there seems no particular reason why a healthy elderly person should not visit a child with chicken pox, nor a healthy child visit a greatgrandparent with shingles. The only circumstance where there is an obvious danger is where one or other is on immunosuppressive therapy, because then the risk of a severe infection is very real. However, simple precautions such as using separate towels are always worth taking.

Figure 12: Herpes Ophthalmicus

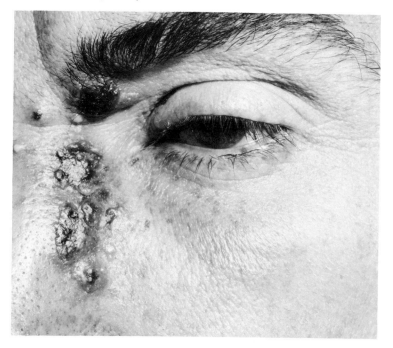

Source: Department of Medical Illustration. St Bartholomew's Hospital, London

**Symptoms**

Herpes ophthalmicus follows the same general course as shingles affecting other parts of the body. A few days of generally increasing but very variable pain along the path of the affected nerve is followed by the typical outbreak of blisters or vesicles round the eye (Figure 12). Most of these have appeared by the end of the second day, but a few new ones may occur up to a week after the first. The pain often abates after the appearance of the rash but it seems to linger longer in herpes ophthalmicus than is general in other sites; in some cases it persists for weeks or months after the rash has disappeared. This may be very hard for elderly people to bear, especially if they are frail.

After a week or so, the vesicles begin to dry up and crust over and they fade away completely leaving no more than minimal scarring provided they have not become secondarily infected by some other organism. The nerve affected — the ophthalmic division of the trigeminal nerve — sends several branches to the area round the eye but only one of these, the nasociliary branch supplying the side of the nose, has any substantial involvement with the eye itself. So in most cases of herpes ophthalmicus affecting the supratrochlear and supraorbital branches of the nerve, only the skin of the forehead and upper eyelid is affected, and the eye itself escapes. It is only where a rash appears under the eye and along the side of the nose that there is danger of involvement. The early signs are swelling eyelids with stickiness along the margins, redness, fluid exudate and, of course, the appearance of vesicles on the conjunctiva and cornea. These may be followed by ulceration and, later, the deposition of fatty material in residual scar tissue, which can lead to permanently compromised sight.

The hardest aspect of herpes ophthalmicus to manage is undoubtedly the long-standing post-herpetic pain (when it occurs); it can be most debilitating in the old. Most other manifestations are either self-limiting or avoidable, although a specialist assessment is advisable in each case, if necessary on a domicillary basis. Simple antibiotic drops may be used to protect the eye from secondary infection, but steroid drops and ointments should never be used, at least until all possibility of an ulcer of the cornea has been excluded.

Diminished corneal sensation may sometimes persist until long after the rash has settled — an 'anaesthetic' eye is much more liable to damage and to the secondary effects of damage than one retaining full sensation; an eyepatch for use out of doors may be advisable.

The manifestations of herpes zoster are not always confined to the sensuary system: local paralysis can also occur and it is generally supposed that the virus is one of the causes of Bell's palsy. This is a fairly sudden paralysis of the muscles of one side of the face due to involvement of the facial nerve as it passes through its bony canal near the ear. It is not uncommon in late life and if the eyelids are affected and cannot close, the eye is exposed to all those chance insults that the lids are designed to guard against. The chief danger is corneal damage and inflammation (keratitis): again, prophylactic antibiotic drops may well be useful. Bell's palsy is usually self-limiting, although there is often a residual weakness especially in the elderly, but this does not usually affect the eyelids to the point where they cannot close. If, occasionally, it does, then specialist referral is indicated, and tarsorraphy (a partial stitching together of the lids) may have to be considered for the eye's proper protection.

## Entropion and Ectropion

Common among elderly people is a tendency of the eyelids to turn inwards (entropion) or outwards (ectropion). Entropion (Figure 13) is usually the result of alteration in the 'tone' of the muscles of the eyelid as well, perhaps, as a decrease in the superficial fat surrounding the eye, which tends to make it fall back into its socket. When the eyelid, either upper or lower or both, turns inward it brings the lashes into contact with the sensitive conjunctiva, setting up a chronic inflammation, as well as increasing the reflex spasm of the muscles. The condition is irritating and uncomfortable and may lead to permanent corneal scarring and a reduction in vision, if severe. Temporary relief may sometimes be obtained by using a small piece of paper suture or 'selotape' to evert the lower lid, though this is seldom possible with the upper lid. There are several simple operative techniques for the relief of entropion that usually produce very good results without undue trouble to the elderly; but the patient must be referred before permanent scarring has occurred.

Figure 13: Entropion

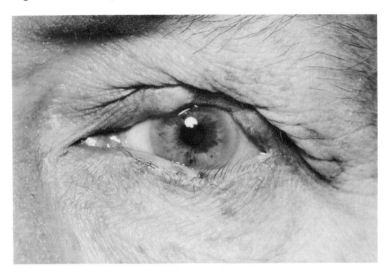

Source: Department of Medical Illustration, St Bartholomew's Hospital, London

Ectropion (Figure 14) is a turning out and down of the lower lid following a gradual weakening of the muscles. The early effect is to compromise the drainage of tears through the punctum, which is no longer in contact with the conjunctiva and which may become inflamed and even blocked. Tears flow freely down the face and are constantly wiped away using a downward and outward motion. This further stretches the already lax tissues of the lower lid and may set up a chronic inflammation or even infection; the situation becomes steadily worse.

Once again, operative cure is both simple and effective and, although elderly people are less likely to have their sight compromised by ectropion than entropion, there is no reason at all why so many of them should have to bear the long-term discomfort, not to say the stigma, that both these unsightly conditions bring.

Figure 14: Ectropion

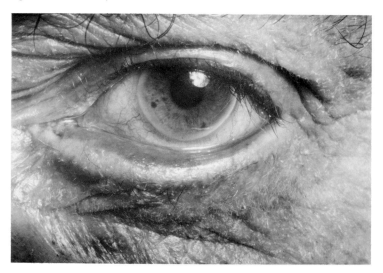

Source: Department of Medical Illustration, St Bartholomew's Hospital, London

## References

1. Ederer, F. (1977/78) 'The Framingham Eye Study', *Blindness American Association of Workers for the Blind, Inc. Annual*, Washington DC
2. Cullinan, T. R. (1977) 'The Epidemiology of Visual Disability. Studies of Visually Disabled People in the Community'. *University of Kent, HSRU Report No. 28*
3. Fenton, P. *et al.* (1975) 'Evaluation of Vision in Slow Stream Wards', *Age and Ageing*, vol. 4 p. 43
4. Gibson, R. and Sanderson, H. (1980) 'Observer Variation in Ophthalmology', *British Journal of Ophthalmology*, vol. 64, pp. 457–60
5. Sperduto, R. *et al.* (1981) 'Lens Opacities and Senile Maculopathy', *Arc. Ophthalmol.*, vol. 99, pp. 1004–8
6. Dobree, J. and Boulter, E. (1982) *Blindness and Visual Handicap. The Facts*, Oxford University Press, New York, Toronto
7. Sarks, S. (1980) 'Drusen and their Relationship to Senile Macular Degeneration', *Australian Journal of Ophthalmology*, vol. 8, pp. 117–30
8. Sarks, S. (1980) 'Ageing and Degeneration in the Macular Region: a Clinico-Pathological Study', *British Journal of Ophthalmology*, vol. 60, pp. 324–41
9. Lovie-Kitchin, J. *et al.* (1982) *Senile Macular Degeneration: The Effects and Management*, Department of Optometry, Queensland Institute of Technology, Brisbane

10. Keen, M. and Jarrett, J. (1981) *Complications of Diabetes*, Edward Arnold, London
11. Goldstein, H. (1968) *The Demography and Causes of Blindness*, The American Foundation for the Blind Inc., New York

# 5 DIAGNOSING VISUAL DISABILITY IN ELDERLY PEOPLE

With perhaps the exception of the relatively rare incipient closed-angle glaucoma and retinal detachments, there are no *urgent* medical reasons why the common sight-threatening diseases of later life should be diagnosed in their earliest possible stages. They do not do damage beyond the eyes and sight loss is seldom sudden. But because the disabilities they lead to are often profound, and because so much can now be done to avert their sometimes slow, but usually inexorable, progress, it is most important that they are found before vision is lost.

Once sight is gone, and with it independence and mobility, it cannot be regained, though very much can be done to maximise what is left. The importance of early diagnosis also extends beyond the performance and enjoyment of visual tasks; Brocklehurst[1] has shown how frequently falls leading to severe fractures are associated with poor vision in elderly people, and there is growing evidence that early confusional states may be enhanced by diminished sensory imput.

The barriers to early diagnosis of visual disability are many, but most can be overcome with surprising ease. The first is the common belief among elderly people that poor sight is an inevitable concomitant of old age and that nothing can be done about it,[2] added, sometimes, to a conviction that 'tired eyes' need subdued lighting and rest, rather than use. There is ample evidence that both these ideas prevent many elderly people from 'bothering' their doctors about their eyes,[3] but the belief that 'eyes are not the doctor's problem' and, in some, the awful fear of going blind, may pose an equal bar. Also, in at least half of elderly visually disabled people, poor vision is accompanied by another severe handicap and, this being of more moment to the patient and the doctor, it may override all considerations of sight. Over half of those people in the community aged 75 years and over (a total of some 3.1 million in the UK in 1981) have some longstanding illness, other than poor sight, that limits them in their daily activities;[4] only when poor sight is the sole handicap does it play a major part in perceived difficulties.[3]

But there are formidable professional barriers to understanding, as well. Most doctors, both outside and inside hospitals,[5] are shy of diagnosing eye disease and even of measuring sight; they feel that it is specialist business and needs specialist equipment. This undoubtedly stems from an undergraduate experience poor in the teaching of ophthalmology and, perhaps even more, during the last 100 years vision has increasingly been seen as the exclusive province of opticians for spectacles, and ophthalmologists for eye disease.[6] The effect has been to lift responsibility for eyesight from the generalist, and to an extent mystify it.[7]

Undoubtedly, adequate diagnosis both for prescription and treatment must be made by those with the expertise and equipment to accomplish it, but it is up to members of the general caring professions and, indeed, relatives of the elderly, to be aware of who needs such expertise and to ensure that they get it. This applies equally to doctors and nurses in hospital, since most visually disabled elderly people with some other significant handicap consult their doctor or go to a specialist outpatient department at least once a year, yet seldom does anybody ask them about their eyesight.[3]

Nevertheless, it is salutory to be reminded of how relatively few elderly people are in regular contact with members of the caring professions (Figure 15). In a survey of one general practice in North London, one in four visually disabled people of 75 years or more had had no contact with an optician or eye specialist for at least five years, and 15 per cent for at least 10 years. Eleven per cent had either never seen an optician or not seen one for over 20 years.[8]

**Simple Steps To Diagnosis**

By far the most important step is the first one — breaking the barriers of silence. Whatever an elderly person's apparent problems, he needs the best vision available to be able to cope — and he needs those who profess to help him to be interested in achieving it. So any conversational approach on the lines of 'How well can you see?', without at first being more specific, breaks the barriers and challenges the taboos that surround the subject.

From that moment any assessment and help should be strictly in terms of the individual's needs — perceived and real — and not

Figure 15: Contact with Caring Services

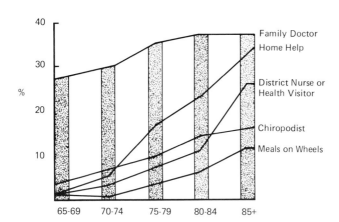

Source: General Household Survey 1981

according to some predetermined formula with rigid cut-off points. Nevertheless, if the answer to the initial question is 'Quite well, thank you', it is worth probing a little further because an elderly person may well be comparing his or her ability to what he supposes is normal for advanced years, or perhaps to some poorly sighted neighbour or friend. This may fall far short of the ideal, or of what can easily be achieved. So questions directed to what is actually being managed, on a near vision (reading, sewing, and so on) and distant vision (mobility inside and outside the house, watching television) basis, are always worth asking. The sensitivity in asking them and in accepting the answers need not be stressed.

If there is any indication that sight is impaired, the administering of simple tests is easy and non-intrusive. Both aspects of acuity should be tested, although there are several points to be remembered in doing so.

*Lighting*

Light is essential for sight, and good light is essential for good sight. It is easy to achieve adequate testing conditions in almost every home with an ordinary reading lamp and a 60 watt bulb[9] —but these are often not the conditions under which an elderly person is trying to manage. How much they matter is discussed in Chapter 7, but in essence the test card (or the newspaper) being used as a near vision test must be viewed with the light coming from over the shoulder and, of course, held at an angle that does not produce glare. An overhead light source is best for the hand-held Snellen chart, again being careful of glare.

### Corrective Lenses

Elderly people are considerably more likely to have approximately adequate correction for near vision than for distant vision though, in the majority, it probably needs updating.[3] Thus, questions related to when glasses were last changed are useful and it is, of course, essential to see that lenses are as clean as possible. The poorly sighted person cannot see how dirty and scratched her lenses are; cleaning them may turn out to be all the help she needs.

### Figure 16: Graduated Print Book for Testing Near Vision

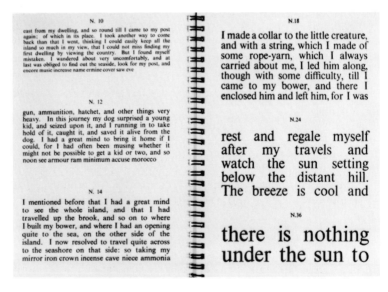

N. 10

east from my dwelling, and so round till I came to my post again; of which in its place. I took another way to come back than that I went, thinking I could easily keep all the island so much in my view, that I could not miss finding my first dwelling by viewing the country. But I found myself mistaken. I wandered about very uncomfortably, and at last was obliged to find out the seaside, look for my post, and encore music increase name ermine cover saw eve

N. 12

gun, ammunition, hatchet, and other things very heavy. In this journey my dog surprised a young kid, and seized upon it, and I running in to take hold of it, caught it, and saved it alive from the dog. I had a great mind to bring it home if I could, for I had often been musing whether it might not be possible to get a kid or two, and so noon see armour ram minimum accuse morocco

N. 14

I mentioned before that I had a great mind to see the whole island, and that I had travelled up the brook, and so on to where I built my bower, and where I had an opening quite to the sea, on the other side of the island. I now resolved to travel quite across to the seashore that side: so taking my mirror iron crown incense cave niece ammonia

N.18

I made a collar to the little creature, and with a string, which I made of some rope-yarn, which I always carried about me, I led him along, though with some difficulty, till I came to my bower, and there I enclosed him and left him, for I was

N.24

rest and regale myself after my travels and watch the sun setting below the distant hill. The breeze is cool and

N.36

there is nothing under the sun to

*Vision Testing*

There is a good argument for making simple sight test cards freely available to anyone who wants them; probably only in that way will the majority of elderly, visually disabled people in the community get tested at all. They should at least be part of the equipment of district nurses, health visitors, general practitioners and hospital doctors, if not of home helps as well.

The near vision card (Figure 16) is simply a series of phrases or sentences in graduated sizes, supposedly printed in good contrast black on white. The notation is that used traditionally by printers; the original test card, designed in the 1860s, was based on print sizes that happened to be about at the time. It has remained substantially unchanged since.[10] More recently, there have been attempts to standardise cards produced by different manufacturers both in print type (Times New Roman is recommended in the UK) and in using words that do not allow, by such clues as letter tails, inspired guesses to be made.

Little of this matters to the elderly person — if he can read N5 then he can read anything; if N8, most of a well-printed newspaper; if N12, he may be helped by large-print books, but will have considerable difficulty with anything smaller. In general, if an elderly person can do no better than N12 in good light, and has not been to an optician within the last two years, then it is well worth such a visit being made, even if there is no eye disease apparent to the observer and even though distance vision and mobility seem to be adequate.

The distance vision (Snellen) card (Figure 17) is usually used at a distance of six metres (20 feet), but few old people live in rooms of this width; a scaled-down three metre card is more practical for domicillary use. The rationale of the card is much more precise than that of the near vision chart, though there are variations in contrast, letter shape and spacing which can compromise its validity.

The theory is that each letter is of a size that can be contained in a square that produces an angle of five minutes on the retina, and made of lines that produce an angle of one minute when read at the distance appropriate to its size. The notation of 6/6 and so on merely signifies what is achieved compared to what would be achieved by a supposedly 'normal' eye at that distance. An eye reading only the top letter of the chart (6/60) is able to define at six metres what a normal eye can define at 60 metres, and so on. The

Figure 17: Scaled Down Snellen Card for use at 10 Feet
(3 Metres)

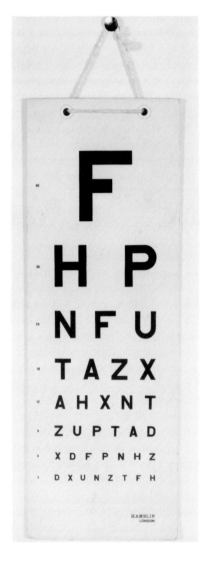

use of letters is a mere convenience — charts using symbols or
pictures have been devised for children and for countries with a
population largely illiterate.

The chart should be held at 10 feet (if scaled down), at the eye level of the seated patient, and tipped a little forward to reduce glare. Each eye should be tested separately and any available 'distance' glasses, with clean lenses, used. A card, or piece of paper, is held over the other eye by the patient. It is best to start at the top and work down and, in general, a complete line with no mistakes after two tries can be taken as the best visual acuity. Anyone with vision of less than 6/18 equivalent has almost certainly got a substantial sight-threatening disease in that eye and should have a specialist opinion. In general, anyone with a visual acuity of 6/9 to 6/18 in the better eye, and who has not been to an optician within the last two years, may very well be helped by a visit. If the optician cannot 'correct' vision to better than 6/18 or suspects eye disease, he will notify the patient's doctor that a specialist opinion is desirable.

## Visual Fields

Loss of peripheral vision, or loss of part of a visual picture, with clear central vision for both near and distant objects is not a common complaint in elderly people. The eye diseases most often responsible — glaucoma and diabetic retinopathy — have usually extended to affect the macula (and thus visual acuity) before a significant disability is noticed. Hemianopia, the loss of vision on the whole of one side, may follow a stroke, of course, but it is rarely unaccompanied by muscle weakness and other symptoms, and these are usually more handicapping than visual loss. Occasionally, a sudden loss of one part of the peripheral visual field may follow a retinal blood vessel thrombosis (clot); but many elderly people, used to circumscribed lives, may not notice it if the other eye is good.

Testing for defects in the peripheral visual field is fairly easy: Gilkes[2] recommends a torch, though a coloured hat pin is equally effective. However, small defects will pass undetected under ordinary conditions. The patient, covering one eye, fixes the gaze of the other onto the eyes of the observer who is about two feet away. The observer then brings the pen torch or hat pin slowly in from one side and crosses to the other, starting at a point where he himself cannot see the light, while he fixates his gaze on the patient's eyes. The manoeuvre is repeated in the vertical plane and the patient is asked to state when she can just see the light, when it disappears and whether there are any positions in which the light cannot be seen. Using this method, it is quite easy to record the 'blind spot' in each eye (the observer's as well as the patient's) opposite where the optic nerve head enters the retina, but it should not affect more than an inch or so of the torch's progress somewhere near the centre of the field.

Such semi-formal testing of visual acuity, and fields, is useful in that it goes a long way towards identifying those who may be in real need of specialist advice, and those in whom help is more likely to be brought about by changes in their environment or in appropriate support. But it reveals little of what the elderly person is actually able to do, visually, in her day-to-day life. The opportunity to accompany her on a shopping expedition may reveal far more. There are so many components of sight — contrast, glare, lighting, print size, colour combinations — that may make daily life very difficult for elderly people and which are not revealed by vision testing either at home or in the more formal surroundings of the consulting room or clinic. All these factors operate much more powerfully outside in public places than in the familiar surroundings of the patient's home. At least two thirds of elderly, visually disabled people have lived in the same house for at least 10 years and so have slowly lost their sight surrounded by the same wallpaper, the same curtains and the same lights.[3]

Finally, it should be remembered that the results obtained from such tests do not accord accurately with the answers to detailed 'closed' questions that have sometimes been suggested, and tried, as a substitute for testing.[3,11] There are so many different meanings implied in the concepts such questions as 'Can you recognise a friend across the street?' introduce, and so many unspoken interactions between young questioner and aged respondent, that this is hardly surprising.

## References

1. Brocklehurst, J. C. *et al.* (1976) 'Fracture of the Femoral Neck, Two Centre Survey of Aetiological Factors' No. 1 June 1976, Departments of Geriatric Medicine, University Hospital of South Manchester and University College Hospital, London
2. Gilkes, M. J. (1978) *Diagnosis of Poor Sight in the Home and the Effects of Various Diseases on Visual Perception*, SWRAB Refresher Course for Specialists in Visual Handicap

3. Cullinan, T. R. (1977) 'The Epidemiology of Visual Disability. Studies of Visually Disabled People in the Community', *University of Kent, HSRU Report No. 28*

4. OPCS (1981) *General Houshold Survey*, Office of Population Census and Surveys, St Catherine's House, London

5. Fenton, P. *et al.* (1975) 'Evaluation of Vision in Slow Stream Wards', *Age and Ageing*, vol. 4, p. 43

6. *Optician's Act* (1958) HMSO, London

7. *Optician's and Competition* (1982) A Report by the Director General of Fair Trading on Section 21 and 25 of the Optician's Act (1958) HMSO, London

8. Calnan, S. (1981) *Elderly People with Poor Sight at Home*(unpublished), Department of Environmental and Preventive Medicine, St Bartholomew's Hospital Medical College, London

9. Cullinan, T. R. *et al.* (1979) 'Visual Disability and Home Lighting', *Lancet*, March 24, vol. 1, pp. 942–4

10. Law, F. (1951) 'Standardization of Reading Types', *British Journal of Ophthalmology*, vol. 35, pp. 765–73

11. Milne, J. S. (1979) 'Longitudinal Studies of Vision in Older People', *Age and Ageing*, vol. 8, pp. 160–6

# 6   SEEKING PROFESSIONAL HELP

For those elderly people newly diagnosed as visually disabled, the first practical step towards help may be through the ophthalmic optician, though this in no way discounts changes that may be needed in the home (see Chapter 7).

Opticians fall into two main categories: ophthalmic opticians who both test sight (in all its parameters) and fit and supply optical appliances, and dispensing opticians who merely dispense lenses and optical appliances.Both are governed by The General Optical Council established under the Opticians Act (1958).[1] Among other duties the Council has the responsibility to maintain high standards and to take steps against practitioners who fall short of these standards. All qualified opticians must be registered with the Council if they wish to practise, and to have their names included on a list held by the local Family Practitioner Committee.[2]

As well as services obtained through opticians, who depend of course on business profit for their livelihood, they can also be obtained through ophthalmic medical practitioners, who contract to supply the ophthalmic services incumbent upon the district health authority. These medical practitioners have all satisfied the appropriate committee of the British Medical Association that they have the experience and qualifications to provide general ophthalmic services under the Health Services Act (1980).[2] Terms of service require an ophthalmic practitioner to make such examinations as may be required and to 'exercise proper care and attention in doing so'. The medical ophthalmic service was set up in 1948 as a temporary measure to overcome the expected rush for ophthalmic and optical services suddenly provided free; it was thought that an expanded hospital service would eventually be able to cope, once the initial surge was over. But the demand was far greater than anticipated[2] and, with an ageing and generally more 'aware' society, has remained so. Thus the complementary services remain, though they now (1981) cost proportionally less than they have ever done (some 5 per cent of total spending on Family Practitioner Services, which itself consumes about 23 per cent of total NHS expenditure (Figure 18).

Figure 18: Percentage of Total National Health Service Expenditure on Different Aspects of Family Practitioner Services

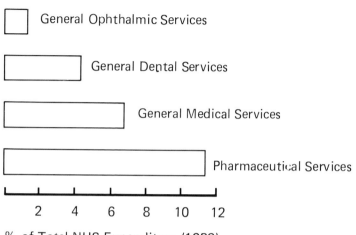

% of Total NHS Expenditure (1983)

Under General Optical Council rules (1960) an ophthalmic medical practitioner or an ophthalmic optician is required to inform a patient's general practitioner if:

1. No optical appliance is required;
2. He detects any abnormality of the eyes or any other condition requiring treatment outside the general ophthalmic services;
3. The patient will not be able to see satisfactorily even with corrective lenses;
4. The patient should be re-examined within six months.

The practical sense in making one of these services a first resort for an elderly person with visual disability is obvious and appointments can usually be made quickly. It is encumbent upon both ophthalmic opticians and ophthalmologists to perform a good eye test, but how far they search for disease appears to vary considerably. Doubtless it partly depends on the visual acuity achieved after lens correction[3] — two recent studies have suggested that between 3 per cent and 11 per cent of all those (including children) having an eye test were referred to a hospital or general practitioner for one of the reasons listed above. In one of the studies, 19 per cent of referrals were for cataract, 8 per cent for macular degeneration and 11 per cent for 'glaucoma'.[2]

Given adequate correction to above 6/18 in the better eye and satisfactory near vision, it is arguable whether further referral to a hospital specialist is justifiable in an elderly person with eye disease, especially if there is some other profound handicap present. The decision is properly that of the general practitioner and his patient, but the doctor may find himself more persuasive when faced with a proliferative diabetic retinopathy with its attendant risk of sudden haemorrhage or with glaucoma, than with a simple cataract or macular degeneration for which little may need doing at this level of acuity. He will be aware how long the local hospital waiting lists are both for an outpatient ophthalmic appointment and for treatment; in the country as a whole, they are measured in months rather than weeks.[3]

In a study in Birmingham, not more than 15 per cent of elderly people referred to the hospital with a (confirmed) diagnosis of cataract were recommended for cataract extraction — the only available treatment.[4] There can be few arguments for adding elderly people to what is now an overburdened system, especially if they have other handicaps as well, unless some positive good is available in the reasonably short term, or unless regular specialist follow-up will lead to that good.

Domiciliary ophthalmic assessments for those unable to reach an optician or ophthalmic practitioner are feasible and have advantages as well as disadvantages. Clearly, they are mandatory for the housebound with visual disability, and important assessments of lighting and low vision aids suitable to the patient and her surroundings can be made during them. But it is rarely possible to make a complete visual assessment, including visual fields, in home conditions. Moreover, opticians are reimbursed only for their travelling expenses in making domiciliary visits and not for their time, though many are prepared to provide the service at loss to themselves.[5] Hospital eye specialists, like all hospital consultants, are available (and paid) for home visits at the request of the general practitioner.

## Hospital Treatment

### Cataract

Cataract treatment is at present always surgical. Great strides have been made from the old days of 'couching' (still extensively practised in many developing countries) and now most operations entail the surgical removal of the whole lens, either with or without its capsule. A new technique in which the lens is broken up and sucked out through a much smaller incision than is generally needed for traditional extraction is being developed. If successful, it should reduce the time spent in hospital and even prove feasible for general outpatient (day-patient) use.

The most important immediate complication of cataract extraction is haemorrhage: the risk of this may necessitate an elderly person spending several days at rest in hospital after operation. But the difficulties in recovering good, useful vision may also be formidable and often need a great deal of specialist and general support over several months if they are to be overcome.

The eye does not settle down to its final refractive state for three or four months after lens removal, and vision in the operated (now 'aphakic') eye and its unoperated fellow is widely dissimilar. Until recently, there has been no way in which such dissimilarity could be resolved without the provision of an accommodating lens that has to be very thick and, because the final refractive state is delayed, reassessed and remade when the eye has 'settled'. Such lenses result in considerable image distortion (Figure 19) and may produce a difference in image size between the two eyes of 20 to 25 per cent,[6] far more than the brain can reconcile. Even when the eye has 'settled down' and final corrective lenses can be prescribed, distortion continues and, with the weight of the lenses, leads many elderly people to become disillusioned and to give up wearing their aphakic lenses.[6]

These and other considerations have inspired the rapid development of contact and implanted lenses. Although contact lenses, especially the new 'permanent' soft type, have many advantages in younger patients, they are less suitable for the elderly because it takes a long time for the patient to become used to them and they need frequent removal and replacement during the initial period — a difficult thing to do with arthritic fingers and, perhaps, trembling hands. Recent evidence has suggested, too, that the image size difference between eyes with and without contact lenses

Figure 19: Distortion Created by Aphakic Lens

The Bank of England.

(i)  As seen normally

(ii) As seen through the eyes of a patient wearing cataract glasses.
The central vision appears larger and nearer than it actually is.
The side vision is bowed and outside this there is a ring area of no
vision at all.

Source: Reproduced With Kind Permission of Mr S. P. B. Percival

(about 9 per cent) is still too much for many individuals to fuse.[6] Implanted, intraocular lenses (Figure 20) hold out far more promise and are now widely used in the United States following the removal of 'senile cataract'. Sight usually settles down in a month or so.

Figure 20: Implanted Lenses in Common Use

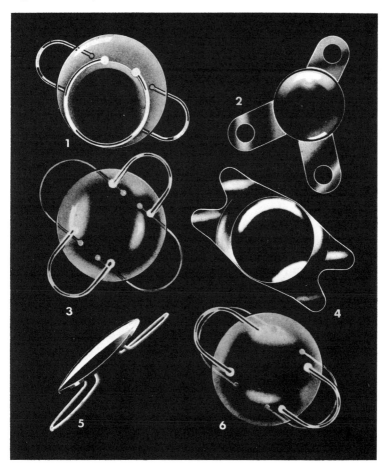

Source: Reproduced With Kind Permission of Mr S. P. B. Percival

## Macular Degeneration

Until recently, there has been no effective treatment for senile macular degeneration; the best that could be done was to enhance such vision as remained. But there has now been considerable promise in laser techniques, which at best arrest or at least delay the inexorable process of sight loss.[7] The technique is much the same as that used in diabetic retinopathy: intense light burns are pinpointed onto the minute areas of new vessel formation, coagulating them and preventing the leakage and oedema that do so much damage. Unfortunately, only a limited range of macular degeneration is amenable to this treatment,[8] and it is at present carried out in only a few centres. It is axiomatic that, at present, most elderly people visually disabled by macular degeneration are not in easy reach of surgical help.

## Diabetic Retinopathy

Judgements about when diabetic retinopathy — either background retinopathy, proliferative retinopathy or maculopathy —is suitable for photocoagulation can be made only by experienced ophthalmologists. However, it is important that all diabetic patients with visible retinopathy should be seen by a specialist and regularly followed. When the diagnosis is made as a result of referral for visual disability, it is essential that they are seen quickly, as even simple background retinopathy is more likely to proceed rapidly to visual loss in the elderly than in the young.[9]

Almost 40 per cent of older people with background retinopathy will have moderate or gross visual impairment within five years of diagnosis, usually because of macular or perimacular involvement rather than gross retinal haemorrhage. Such background retinopathy (like the proliferative variety) is amenable to arrest with photocoagulation when it involves the macula, but there is no evidence that visual loss can be further arrested when vision has fallen to below 6/36; that is why regular assessment is so important. At least yearly retinal examination, with dilated pupil, is advocated for all people with diagnosed diabetes, and six-monthly for assessment and follow-up of visible retinopathy. At any one time, approximately 2 per cent of the population (of average age-spread, with 18 to 20 per cent over the age of 60) will have clinically diagnosable diabetes, and one in 10 of these will have a visible retinopathy.

Although there are many good reasons for striving towards accurate control of diabetes at all ages, there is as yet no incontrovertible evidence that control alone limits either the onset or progress of retinopathy, or determines which of the main types predominate. Other factors such as age of onset, family history and even smoking may play a part. Nevertheless, the success in at least the arrest of progressive visual disability by photocoagulation is undoubted, though services are of necessity concentrated in a few specialist units, and the difficulties that elderly people may have in reaching them are often formidable.

*Glaucoma*

The acute, closed-angle type that leads to a painful red eye, colour distortion and blurring of vision, sometimes accompanied by headache and vomiting, is not very common in elderly people in Great Britain, but constitutes a medical emergency when it occurs. Unless pressure is relieved quickly, sight can easily be lost because the blood supply to the retina is cut off by the sudden rise in pressure within the eye itself. Admission to hospital is always necessary.

Drops (pilocarpine and its derivatives) are used to constrict the pupil and, hopefully, reopen the angle. Acetazolomide (Diamox) is given by mouth to reduce the output of intraocular fluid. An operation is performed to promote drainage from the front part of the eye, when the eye has settled down, by making several small holes in the iris. The other eye is usually operated on at the same time, since 60 per cent of people are likely to suffer an acute attack in the second eye within a year of the first.

The more insidious, chronic, open-angle glaucoma is much harder to diagnose in elderly people and will often have progressed to considerable sight loss before it is recognised. However, pressure within the eyeball is always raised and this can be detected quite easily by most ophthalmic opticians and by all ophthalmologists; though by no means all people with raised pressure in late middle-age will necessarily develop glaucoma. Certainly, anyone with a known family history of glaucoma should be 'screened' regularly from middle-age onwards.

An elderly person should be referred to a specialist for full asessment if chronic glaucoma is suspected or a field loss detected, even without any loss of visual acuity. Medical treatment, either as locally applied drops (such as pilocarpine) or the new Timolol, with or without oral, pressure-lowering, drugs such as an acetazolamide (for example, Diamox) may keep presure down for years and prevent the loss of any more of the visual field. However, a drainage operation may eventually be needed; it is usually effective in relieving high pressure, though not in improving sight once it has been lost.[10]

## References

1. *Optician's Act* (1958), HMSO, London
2. *Opticians and Competiton* (1982), A Report by the Director General of Fair Trading on Sections 21 and 26 of The Optician's Act (1958), HMSO, London
3. London Health Planning Consortium (March 1980) *Report of the Study Group on Ophthalmology Service in the North Thames Regions*
4. Brennan, M. *et al.* (1975) 'The Incidence of Cataract and its Clinical Presentation', *Community Health*, vol. 7, pp. 13–20
5. Calnan, S. (1981) *Elderly People with Poor Sight at Home* (unpublished), Department of Environmental and Preventive Medicine, St Bartholomew's Hospital Medical College, London
6. Vision Research: A National Plan 1978–1982. The 1977 Report of the National Advisory Eye Council, *US Department of HEW, Publication No. (NIH) 78–1258*
7. Gass, J. M. D. (1977) *Stereoscopic Atlas of Macular Diseases — Diagnosis and Treatment*, 2nd ed. C. V. Mosby Co, St Louis
8. Talbot, J. and Bird, A. (1980) 'Krypton Laser in the Management of Disciform Macular Degeneration', *Trans. Ophthalmology Society of the UK*, vol. 100, part 3, pp. 423–4
9. Keen, M. and Jarrett, J. (1981) *Complications of Diabetes*, Edward Arnold, London
10. Dobree, J. and Boulter, E. (1982) *Blindness and Visual Handicap: The Facts*, Oxford University Press, New York, Toronto

# 7 LIGHTING, CONTRAST AND COLOUR

Good sight needs good light; and good light is not only bright light but light tailored to the task and to the individual. Almost subconsciously, younger people, who are able to manipulate their environments, adjust available lighting to their needs. Small objects are carried to the window, furniture is shifted to make use of light, high wattage bulbs and modern spotlights manoeuvred until the best effect is achieved. However, many elderly people live in surroundings that have grown old with them, and what sufficed in youth is seldom enough for old age. Lighting is deficient or inappropriate, or both, in the homes of most elderly people and certainly not enough to provide three times the amount of light to

**Figure 21: Home and Hospital (Eye Clinic) Lighting. Ambient Lighting in the Homes of 56 Elderly People**

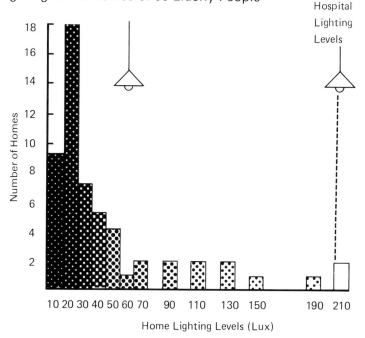

the older retina that the young eye needs to achieve the same resolution.

Figure 21 illustrates the point; it comes from a study of the lighting in the homes of 56 elderly people with very low vision attending a hospital eye clinic.[1] In almost every home, general ambient room lighting (Figure 21) was considerably below the lighting levels used in the hospital clinic for testing distance vision, and in most cases was woefully inadequate for elderly, let alone diseased, eyes. Figure 22 illustrates the findings for near vision tasks. Here the situation is not quite so bad — indeed, two homes had magnificent lighting, well above the hospital standard. But lighting was very poor for the majority — it did not approach the 450 to 600 lux recommended by the Illuminating Engineering Society for elderly people engaged in prolonged reading or sewing.[2]

Figure 22: Home and Hospital (Eye Clinic) Lighting. Near Vision Lighting in the Homes of 56 Elderly People

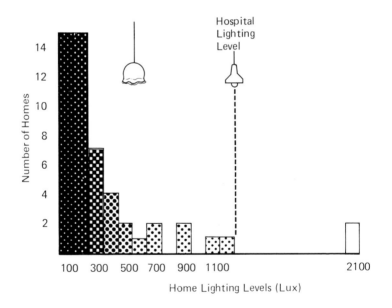

The same study examined the effect that an improvement in home lighting had on the visual acuity of poorly sighted elderly people. It was possible to bring almost all ambient and near illumination up to hospital standards, and in many cases well above, using only a

clean, well positioned 60 watt bulb, and to show that measured visual acuity was improved moderately or markedly in over half of the subjects. Several other studies have demonstrated how the visual acuity of elderly people continues to improve with better lighting after younger eyes have reached their maximum potential.[3,4] Yet old and dirty lampshades, poorly painted walls, low wattage bulbs, half drawn or dirty net curtains and dark light-absorbing furniture often conspire to maintain an elderly person in the worst possible light environment. Two erroneous beliefs also play a part: that 'tired eyes' must be rested in dim light and that bright lights are expensive. The difference between burning a 60 watt and a 40 watt bulb for eight hours every day is little more than 70p per month.

## Lamps and Bulbs

The common filament bulb is woefully inefficient compared to other modern light sources. It gives no more than 12 lumens for every watt burned and converts a great deal of its energy into heat; the low-pressure sodium lamp (such as is used on motorways) gives about 150 lumens per watt. But the filament lamp gives out light in a wide colour band, thus allowing good colour discrimination; the sodium lamp, being restricted to the red-yellow end of the spectrum allows practically none.

New pressure lamps have been developed which give a wider colour range — principally a high-pressure sodium lamp — but they lose a little in efficiency and are not yet adapted to domestic use. The ordinary domestic-type fluorescent mercury lamp produces about 90 lumens per watt, depending on what colour ranges it achieves, but it is generally less suited to elderly people because of its start-up time and because its life is dramatically lessened by frequent (rather than constant) use. The life of such a bulb is quoted as about 7,500 hours, but this may be halved by being switched on and off hourly, and doubled by being left on. In general, this applies also to filament bulbs but *their life expectancy is never quoted* and many cheap bulbs of low standard are imported. However, filament bulbs do have the great advantage of being familiar, and therefore preferred, and of being relatively cheap to buy and easy to change.

## Glare

Glare is experienced when a bright light comes from many different sources at once or is reflected from a broken surface, such as a sunlit sea. It increases rapidly with increasing brightness of the light source, but only slowly with its size, so that a plastic shade round a naked light bulb (which produces glare because of its shape) is effective in reducing uncomfortable glare because it reduces brightness and increases size almost in the same proportion.[5] Of course, the bright interior of a dark reading shade does the same, but although the light produced is focused and pleasant, less than 30 per cent may actually be available, the rest being absorbed or converted into heat.

Glare may be a particular problem for people with cataracts: the effect of the lens changes is to shatter the light passing through and distribute it across the retina in confusion. The effect is even worse if there is glare from the light source or reflected surface. Gilkes[6] makes the useful analogy of driving a car with a dirty windscreen in bright sunlight coming from above — the particles of dirt shatter the light and make it impossible to see. But when going through a tunnel or under trees, the angled light is cut out and the driver can see perfectly well through the dirty screen. That is why many elderly people prefer to live in diffused light, even though they do not have cataracts — and why, as Gilkes says, some old ladies say they see better with their hats on!

## Contrast

Several studies have examined the relationship between lighting levels, task size, image contrasts and visual performance.[4] They have all shown that, while visual acuity goes on improving with increasing light in the elderly after no further improvement can be demonstrated in the young, a level is soon reached in both where nothing more can be achieved without increasing image size or contrast, or both. This should be remembered, even in apparently good lighting conditions; contrast implies not only the depth of colour or black pigment against its background, but also the sharpness of its outline.

In this respect, one should consider how inadequate are many well-loved surfaces, old and new, for fine close work, such as cutting up food, picking up small objects, and so on. A dark surface may reflect only 10 to 20 per cent of light falling on it, whereas a bright white plastic top or table cloth reflects 70 to 80 per cent, and improves the chances of good contrast accordingly.

It is equally important in ambient lighting: the elderly person with failing vision uses the bannister because she knows it is there, not because she can see its dark wood against the equally dark wall behind it. Very many new public buildings, including hospitals, fail to make the colour distinctions on stairs, handrails, doors and so on, which would make life both safer and easier for the elderly. Yet such contrasts can be as attractive as they are intelligent.

Good lighting and colour contrast are also surprisingly often neglected in the much vaunted interiors of the modern so-called ergonomically designed home. The neatly hidden strip lamp beneath the eye level cupboard in the new kitchen throws into shadow the front surface of the objects it is supposed to illuminate, making it impossible for the aged eye to read labels or measures. The surfaces themselves are often of much the same colour as the white porcelain on them. Markings on kitchen dials, washing machines and other modern appliances are very small and in non-contrasting colours, and light switches are made to match the walls, not stand out from them. Modern stair design seldom distinguishes in colour between riser and tread and the point where the stairs end and the landing begins is not easy for the visually disabled eye to discern. Lighting on stairs and in passage ways, though generally brighter than it once was, is no better positioned than in the past, and there is little thought to the colour contrasts of walls and floors. The net effect to the poorly sighted person may be precisely the same as trying to fly an aircraft through a cloud, where all points of visual reference are removed; it becomes difficult even to judge whether one is horizontal, let alone whether one is going straight.

## Improving Conditions

Anyone can assist an elderly person to make simple and very effective improvements in lighting standards and they should not be frightened of doing so. The first step is to decide what he wants to do and then to arrange the best lighting for doing it: attending to details is better than aiming at general improvement.

In this way, necessary changes can be negotiated sensitively, made enjoyable and thus used — rather than being just another worrying intrusion into a treasured self-identity, to be discarded as soon as the well-intentioned do-gooder has gone. In effecting changes it is important to remember the physical law that relates the intensity of light to the square of its distance — in other words, halving the distance of a light source increases illumination four times. This has the greatest practical importance for reading and other near-vision occupations when the light from a table lamp comes from a single source. It is of less relevance in general, ambient room-lighting, which depends much more on reflective surfaces for its transmission, such as walls, ceilings and table tops. In effect, a well placed reading lamp seldom needs more than a 60 watt bulb; 100 watts often generates far more heat than is comfortable and is, anyway, more expensive.

Beware, too, of improving near vision lighting while leaving the rest of the room, stairs and passage ways in relative darkness. Dark accommodation becomes much slower with increasing age so that moving from a bright light to dark leaves the older person virtually blind for a minute or longer. It is important to remember this in respect to watching television as well as reading; the intensity of light from a back-lit television screen is greater than most people ever experience in other domestic situations but to reduce reflection from the surface, or save money, it is still often watched in near dark.

For the daylight hours, a great deal can be achieved by adjusting the position of favourite chairs so that light from the window comes over the shoulder onto the close work. It is within everybody's experience that light falling at right angles onto an object sharply contrasted with its background makes discrimination easiest and, while this may most easily be arranged so that the light comes from behind, it need not necessarily be so. Any position of a favourite chair that enhances both natural and artificial near-vision light and at the same time avoids direct glare through the window, the ever-present danger of trailing wires or the knocking of lamps from side tables, is usually better than one that demands different positions for different tasks during the day. For the same reasons, beds should not face windows nor television sets be placed so that light is reflected from their screens.

A central light source with two or three 60 watt bulbs in a translucent globe is to be preferred for ambient lighting to the modern spot-light arrangements so favoured by the ergonomists. Certainly, the damask-shaded, shadow-producing luminaires that many old people believe is all they can afford are not at all ideal. The effect of lowering the central illumination is much better and cheaper than putting in higher wattage bulbs. Good light-reflecting surfaces are essential and, if possible, crockery, knife handles, bowls, knitting needles, combs and any other familiar everyday objects should be in colours contrasting to the table or work top. Redecoration of walls may be essential, with, if possible, doors, floors, light switches and so on in colours that make them stand out from the walls.

## References

1. Cullinan. T., Silver, J., Gould, E. and Irvine, D. (1979) 'Visual Disability and Home Lighting', *Lancet*, vol. 1, pp. 642–4
2. Illuminating Engineering Society (1977) *IES Code for Interior Lighting*, London
3. Levitt, J. (1978) 'Lighting for the Elderly: An Optician's View' *Proceedings of Symposium Light for Low Vision*, Chartered Institute of Building Services, London
4. Boyce, P. R. (1973) *Lighting Research and Technology*, vol. 5, no.3, p. 125
5. Jay, P. (1978) 'Fundamentals', *Proceedings of Symposium Light for Low Vision*, Chartered Institute of Building Services, London
6. Gilkes, M. (1979) 'Eyes Run On Light', *British Medical Journal*, vol. 1, pp. 1681–3
7. Weale, R. A. (1982) *A Biography of the Eye, Development, Growth, Age*, H. K. Lewis & Co., London

# 8 OPTICAL AIDS IN LOW VISION

Janet Silver
Principal Ophthalmic Optician, Moorfields Eye Hospital, London

After all available treatment has been given a specialist may well refer an elderly patient for assessment to a low-vision clinic. The aim of this assessment is not only to ascertain how much useful vision remains but how the best use can be made of it to help the individual do those things that he or she wants to do. The techniques are very personal and depend as much on the sensitive encouragement as on the high technology of the lens system suggested. The aim is to restore the autonomy and independence, as well as the useful vision of the patient as far as it is possible. There is an enormous loss of privacy and of self-esteem in being unable to read a gas bill or a bank statement and it is a great achievement to restore this ability, even if reading for pleasure is lost.

Most specialist eye hospitals have established low-vision clinics and some will accept referrals from other hospitals. Other areas contract-out to firms of opticians known to have some expertise in this work; in others, a local practitioner accepts 'referrals' on a hospital prescription. Alternatively, the patient herself can ask a general medical practitioner to seek a second opinion and this time ensure that the selected hospital does run a low-vision clinic.

Regrettably, there are still many areas where no service at all is available; then it may be necessary to consult an independent practitioner on a private basis. This can be an expensive procedure since low-vision assessment will take an experienced practitioner up to an hour, the resulting prescription may be for a simple magnifier costing perhaps £5 or a pair of telescopic spectacles which may cost as much as £300.

Perhaps 70 per cent of those referred to a low-vision clinic can be helped substantially by the techniques and aids available. Poor vision is not the limiting factor for the successful use of aids. Theoretically, the patient should be able to read newsprint if he has enough sight to count fingers at arm's length, but it is very important for the patient to understand that no aid will replace the vision that has been lost, and that every aid requires some adaption. The higher the magnification, the greater are the problems involved.

Low vision aids may range from the familiar 'Sherlock Holmes' type magnifier through to complicated electronic machines with built-in intelligence. Aids work by the application of a few very simple principles. They either make an image of the object to be viewed large enough for the visually handicapped person to understand it, or they project an image so large on the retina that, although the image may be degraded, it is still recognisable. Chapter 4 describes the type and effect of different eye diseases leading to visual disability. Most of the people affected are likely to be able to get around with relative ease, but have problems appreciating detail. Typically, they will complain of being unable to recognise an acquaintance in the street or to read small print.

For the largest group, those with central distortion or even a 'hole in the centre', it is often discovered quite spontaneously that looking slightly away from the object actually leads to seeing it better. This technique can be developed by looking at a regularly patterned surface such as a tiled wall or a chess board. It will be seen that with the gaze fixed firmly at the centre, one area (perhaps just above or just below the point of fixation) is relatively clear and undistorted. A poorly sighted person can then practise fixing so that the image falls on a 'good' part of the retina. Like all skills, it becomes easier with practice.

**Type of Aids Available (Figure 23)**

Many people discover for themselves that a simple hand magnifier can give access to smaller print than can be read with ordinary glasses. Hand lenses can be made of plastics or glass, be mounted in metal or plastic rings, be poor quality or good quality, and very cheap or very expensive; the last two factors are not necessarily related. There is a common misconception that a large magnifier is likely to be better than a small one. Indeed, this is occasionally true but large magnifiers are always low-powered. The power of any lens depends on the relationship between the two surfaces. Generally, the more steeply curved (convex) they are the higher the power and, clearly, a large high-powered lens would be enormously difficult to make, require a lot of material, be very heavy and inevitably expensive. Magnifiers are well accepted and fit very readily into an established way of life. While they may often be the only aid a person has, many who use a more sophisticated aid find a little lens very useful for looking at prices in supermarkets, seeing the dials on the gas cooker, reading sets of instructions and so on.

## Figure 23: Optical Aids for Low Vision (Examples)

Top row
1. Keeler binocular near vision spectacles   (magnification × 5)
2. Coil stand magnifier   (magnification × 5)
3. Bioptic telescopic spectacles for distance vision   (magnification × 2)

Middle row
1. Left 'bifocal' spectacle magnifier   (magnification up to 9)
2. Peak loupe illuminated   (magnification × 10)
3. Binoculars, miniature   (magnification × 6)

Bottom row
1. Clip-up spectacle magnifier. Ary loupe
2. Dome magnifier   (magnification × 2)
3. Clip-on telescope. Available for distance and near vision
                              (magnification × 3)
(Photographs courtesy of Miss J. Silver)

Hand-held magnifiers have to be held steadily above the page. Old people can be helped to learn how to judge and sustain this distance. Simple strategies such as supporting an elbow on a cushion on the armchair will often make this much easier. In those whose grip is impaired or who have a tremor, similar magnifiers can be mounted on stands, which control the distance from the page by resting on the book. The higher the magnification, the shorter the distance of the lens from the print, and at higher levels it may be difficult to organise shadow-free light on the print. A number of magnifiers have built-in illumination, usually battery-powered, to solve this problem. While these lenses have literally thousands of uses, they all have the disadvantage that at least one hand is needed to hold them. That particular problem is solved if magnifiers are mounted on a spectacle frame, though the distance-to-page limits still apply. It may be quite difficult to persuade an old person to hold a book perhaps two inches from her nose. There is frequently the fear that holding things close will in some way exacerbate the disease process. In fact, the working distance when using the eyes cannot affect them one way or another, but there is considerable evidence that people with a visual disability do learn to use their residual vision better with practice.

Telescopic lenses are indicated where a longer working distance is needed, such as in sewing or writing. Telescopic lenses create a lot of problems. They can be very heavy, conspicuous and give a limited area of view. The user also gets the impression that objects are nearer because they make things seem so much larger, and therefore there are problems in judging the relationship of one object to another. For example, if a telescope is used when writing, then the pen appears much closer than it actually is. However, apart from a few low-powered magnifiers that can be held on stands or perhaps suspended around the neck, telescopes are the only aid that will allow any task needing both hands and a fairish space. Telescopes make possible such tasks as sewing on a button, doing the crossword puzzle and wiring a plug.

Telescopic lenses can also be used for much greater distances and here their use is more familiar. Many people use opera glasses at the theatre; very few have considered using them in the cinema or to see the station sign in the railway, or the bus number, or the children playing in the garden. Telescopic lenses are frequently requested to use for watching television but the best way to achieve magnification here is simply to move closer. Moving from 10 to three feet from the screen actually gives an effective 3X magnification, with none of the disadvantages of a complex lens system.

The last groups of aids, available only relatively recently, use a television camera to transmit a picture of the print to a television screen. These have many advantages. The person can sit in a relatively normal position with the print mounted on the platform which she moves under the camera. The print can be magnified to any size and, of course, both eyes are used. Further, most patients seem to prefer a white image on a black background and this is readily achieved with closed circuit television (CCTV). The disadvantages are that the machine is bulky, cannot be readily moved around and, at the time of writing, costs anything form £1,000 upwards. CCTVs can be wired up to computers and allow word processing and other computer techniques.

Through the hospital service, all low-vision aids are issued on an 'on loan' basis. Aids are recovered when they are no longer the most appropriate and can often be used again. Frequently, at an early assessment, the patient may not be ready to adapt to the ideal aid, but it is possible to advance to more complex ones after she has become used to using simple aids. Also, of course, all the patient's needs may not be recognised at the first visit and further aids may be introduced, or the original aids modified, when these become better understood.

A good low-vision practitioner will often prefer to assess the patient on his own because communication is much better that way. At the end of the interview the escort can be shown the correct reading position, the correct illumination levels and have the problems explained. An old person who might be confused can then be reminded at home that the aid demands, for instance, a short working distance and a repositioning of the light source.

Family and friends play an important role in helping someone with low vision to gain optimum benefit from her residual vision and her aids. First, she needs reassurance that the demands she is making on her eyes will not damage them. She is likely to get most discouraged about the use of the aids; most people find it difficult to modify many years of doing things one way. Messages about working distances and illumination need strong reinforcement. However, once the new tricks are learned then life becomes much simpler, and its quality considerably enhanced.

# 9 VOLUNTARY AND STATUTORY HELP

Anyone seeking to help an elderly person with failing vision will soon find herself embroiled in the process of marshalling the many different organisations and services that set out to help handicapped people. The plethora of possibilities makes it most unlikely that any but the most mentally and physically agile of old people could manage by themselves. The dearth over most of the country of health visitors and social workers with particular responsibilities for the elderly makes it essential that as many people as possible are aware of what can be done and how to go about doing it. This includes, of course, the sensitive use of 'appropriate technology' — appropriate, that is, to the whole needs and capabilities of each individual, rather than a shower of smart, slick and unusable gadgets.

Most of the voluntary or charitable bodies concerned specifically with visual disability have declared traditionally their interest to be in 'the blind', as statutorily defined. The Royal National Institute for The Blind (RNIB) is the main national organisation, but there are also national groupings of people with special interests such as retinitis pigmentosa or children who are both blind and deaf. More locally, there are very many voluntary associations and societies, arranged on a geographical basis, devoted to the interests of 'the blind'. The RNIB publishes a comprehensive list of names and addresses (price £5), but they are also in local telephone directories and at Citizens Advice Bureaux. These voluntary bodies are loosely grouped under the umbrella of regional associations, one for the north and one, combined, for the south and west of the UK.

The local associations vary in the extent to which they are able and willing to offer help to those with a visual disability who are not registered as 'blind' or, occasionally, as 'partially sighted'. Most of them recognise that there is a need but feel that they must be restrictive because both their funds and facilities are limited. However, this should not deter anyone from making an approach.

Traditionally, the voluntary associations have spearheaded the application of new ideas both in training and rehabilitation of 'blind people', but in 1971 they lost much of their rehabilitative role to local authorites who took on statutory responsibility for all handicapped people in the country. This left some local associations for the 'blind' unsure of the part they had to play and a few have tended to revert to the old charitable image of simply raising money and using it solely for Christmas parties and outings — very much the 'them and us' approach which leads to stigma and stagnation.[1] Others have found it difficult to work closely with local authorities, each being jealous of the old and new concepts that should truly unite volunteers and professionals. Specifically, some local authorities have been reluctant to pass on information about registered 'blind' people in need, feeling it to be a breach of confidence. But there are some local associations that have developed a new dynamic, often of course by directly involving 'blind' people in their direction and management. A few (such as Warwick) have even become the agents of the local authority in carrying out its statutory duty. This close association of voluntary and professional workers has much to offer in meeting, sensitively, all the complex needs of handicapped eldery people — the professional has the expertise and the volunteer the time to give the support that is always needed. Such a combination can be enhanced by offering specialised training to volunteers.[2]

In an effort to mobilise resources for visually disabled people who are not registered as blind, a national Partially Sighted Society has been formed with local branches up and down the country. It has not yet had time to develop its full strength and, like all young movements, must spend much of its time in making itself heard. The society publishes a regular magazine, *Oculus*, which gives news of local branch meetings as well as more general news of interest. It depends entirely on voluntary help and has no local salaried staff, unlike some of the larger blind welfare associations. Together with the Electricity Council, the Partially Sighted Society has produced a very useful booklet on lighting and low vision that can be obtained from their Midlands office. Helpful advice on home lighting is also obtainable from the Optical Information Council and through some local electricity showrooms.

Centrally, the RNIB, with an annual income of some £9,000,000, stimulates and commissions research and technical development, runs residential homes and training establishments, maintains a very comprehensive library both in print and in

Braille, a publishing house and a direct order facility for all the prosthetics and aids that are of such help to 'blind' people. It was founded in 1848 and has numerous branches throughout the country. Although most emphasis is on the registered 'blind', many of its ideas and facilities are of use and benefit to the 'visually disabled' as well. A comprehensive list of leaflet publications, most of which are free, may be obtained on request to central or branch offices. Among the most useful are *Hints for Blind Housewives*, which contains many examples of simple gadgets and techniques equally suitable to those with a visual disability and, indeed, non-visual handicap, and *Useful Articles Sold in Shops or by Mail Order*, which is a full list of simple aids, gadgets and safety devices sold in ordinary shops throughout the country.

The 400 and more specially designed or adapted goods that the RNIB itself sells are offered at concessionary price to those registered as 'blind' and at full price to others. Although many of the simpler devices, for both daily living and leisure (for example very large print playing cards), are obviously attractive to a wide range of visually disabled elderly people, it must be said that much of the 'high technology' is not. It has been designed very much with education and employment in mind, and the techniques to be learned before it can be used successfully are usually beyond the interest of people in their retirement years. However, the RNIB is developing an outward-looking stance and is increasingly aware of the needs of visually disabled elderly people who may well not be registerable as blind, as well as continuing its invaluable traditional role in education and training. All approaches are welcomed.

Almost all major public libraries now carry a range of books in large print and a full list of what is available may be had from the major publishers (see list of addresses at end). The range is far more comprehensive and exciting than it used to be and is ever-expanding; demands on public libraries are the best way of stimulating their growth. Very few elderly 'blind' people read Braille or even the simpler Moon alphabet; in fact, no more than 10 per cent in a 1965 survey of elderly 'blind' people could do so.[3] In this same survey, 77 per cent said they had never had a 'talking book' (many claiming lack of interest or to 'prefer the wireless'), but this service has developed considerably since the date of the survey and its coverage among the 'blind' at least must now be much wider than it was then. Talking books are provided from two main sources — the British Talking Book Service and CALIBER.

The Talking Book Service is supplied free to those registered as blind or partially sighted; other visually disabled people may become members at an annual subscription of £15.40 and an application form signed by an ophthalmologist, GP or ophthalmic optician confirming that they have defective reading vision (generally no better than N12). The current catalogue is very extensive.

The *In Touch* programme on BBC is too well-known to need further description and many local radio stations provide a similar programme on a regular basis dealing with local news. Many of them also organise a taped news service; Radio London has a list of services supplying cassette tapes nationally for various interest groups, on health, gardening and so on.

The Disabled Living Foundation (DLF), which concerns itself with making life easier for all the disabled, has devoted a considerable amount of its resources to visually disabled people. There is a permanent exhibition of devices and gadgets at its headquarters in Harrow Road, London, but an appointment should be made before a visit is paid. Especially interesting is its new 'model kitchen', designed in co-operation with *In Touch*, which displays the truly amazing range of gadgets and devices that have been designed to make life easier and safer for poorly sighted people. Although many ideas are likely to spring from a visit to the DLF, especially if it is made by, or on behalf of, someone with more than one handicapping condition, it is as well to have a very clear picture of what is really wanted before the visit is made. So wide is the choice that muddle can easily ensue: the devices are designed for the disablility, not the other way round.

The DLF also acts as a pressure group to mitigate the lot of handicapped people, and it has recently achieved a great deal in getting supermarket labelling and official forms made more legible both in print size and colour contrast. It publishes many useful leaflets, obtainable on application. Of special interest is the comprehensive list of low-vision services available in the UK, the list of suppliers (and prices) of optical aids and magnifiers, and an interesting list of large-print sheet music available from various sources. Many of the aids available from the DLF are also, of course, available through local authority social service departments or voluntary associations and quite a few can be bought in local shops; but it is very instructive to see the huge range of possibilities under one roof. The DLF also runs regular training courses for both professionals and volunteers in all aspects of handicap.

## Statutory Services

Local authorities discharge their responsibilities to visually handicapped people through social workers and the provision of technical and other aids. Normally, only those registered as 'partially sighted' or 'blind' are brought to their attention. Some areas have retained social workers with special training and responsibility for 'blind' people and some have redevolved responsibility to voluntary associations, often paying the salary of a specialised worker. In other parts, mobility officers for the 'blind' are employed with special responsibility for training blind people in getting out and about and shopping, for example. But in other areas services are slight and there are few social workers with special training and interest. In any case, they are available only to those who are registered, unlike mobility officers who will undertake to help anyone with failing sight. It must also be stressed that almost all studies have shown that elderly, visually disabled people experience more difficulties inside their own homes than in getting about outside them; mobility is more often restricted by some other handicap.

However, local authorities offer many other services that may be of help to visually disabled people and an approach through the occupational therapy service will often be useful. Help with hand and bath rails, cooking aids, crockery, lighting and telephones may all be available, for instance, as well as much advice about extra benefits, and help with rates and heating. Many hospital ophthalmic clinics also employ their own social workers who, on home visits, can best advise about the proper use of post-operative and other aids, as well as mobilising the sort of help an elderly person will need to make best use of residual vision.

Such a large range of possibilities must at first seem daunting to anyone trying to help an elderly person with visual problems. Indeed, their very diversity speaks of past failures and poor thinking; but it also speaks of a willingness to go on trying and this willingness, both local and national, is much easier to tap than at first seems believable. However, in doing so a few basic rules are well worth following:

1. The helper must be absolutely sure of what it is an elderly person wants to do that cannot already be done;
2. The simplest way of doing it must be found;
3. Continuing encouragement and help must be provided and of the sort necessary to get used to any new techniques.

These simple rules may seem obvious but it is because they are so often forgotten that so many 'aids' lie about unused and redundant.

## References

1. Armstrong, J. D. (1978) 'The Future Role of Voluntary Associations' in *Regional Review*, Southern and Western Regional Association for the Blind, vol. 63, Spring 1978
2. Casswell, G. N. Address: Southampton College of Technology, Southampton, Hants
3. Gray, P. G. and Todd, J. (1965) *Mobility and Reading Habits of the Blind*, Government Social Survey, HMSO, London

# ADDRESSES

ADA Reading Service for the Blind
6 Dalewood Rise, Lavestock, Salisbury, Wilts
Tel: 0722–26987

Age Concern
Bernard Sunley House
60 Pitcairn Road, Mitcham, Surrey, CR4 3LL
Tel: 01–640 5431

Birmingham Royal Institute for the Blind
49 Court Oak Road, Birmingham 17,
Tel: 021–427 1066

British Broadcasting Corp
Publications, PO Box 234, London, SE1 3TH

British Diabetic Association
10 Queen Anne Street, London, W1
Tel: 01–323 1531

British Lighting Council
16–18 Lancaster Place, London WC2

British Retinitis Pigmentosa Society
Secretary : Mrs L Drummond Walker,
Greensnorton Court
Greensnorton, Towcester, Northants
Tel 0327–53276

British Talking Book Service for the Blind
Mount Pleasant, Alperton, Wembley, Middlesex HA0 1RR
Tel: 01–903 6666

BWBF British Wireless for the Blind Fund
224 Great Portland Street, London, W1N 6AA
Tel: 01–388 1266

CALIBER Cassette Library for Blind and Handicapped
Aylesbury, Bucks, HP 1HU

Cedric Chivers Ltd, Book Sales Division
93–100 Locksbrook Road, Bath, Avon, BA1 3HB

Consumers Association
14 Buckingham Street, London, WC2
Tel: 01–839 1222

Directory of Agencies for the Blind, price £5.00, RNIB

Disabled Living Foundation
380–384 Harrow Road, London, W9 2HU
Tel: 01–289 6111

Disability Alliance
25 Denmark Street, London, WC2
Tel: 01–240 0806

Family Welfare Association
501–505 Kingsland Road, Dalston, London, E8 4AU
Tel: 01–254 6251

Greater London Fund for the Blind
2 Wyndham Place, London, W1
Tel 01–262 0191

Guide Dogs for the Blind
Association
Alexandra House, 113 Uxbridge
Road, Ealing, London, W5
Tel: 01–567 7001

Illuminating Engineering Society
York House, Westminster
Bridge Road, London, SE1

'In Touch', BBC
Broadcasting House, London,
W1A 1AA

Irish National Council for the Blind
10 Lower Hatch Street, Dublin 2
Tel: Dublin 76–10–08

Irish National League of the Blind
35 Gardiner Place, Dublin 1
Tel: Dublin 74–27–92

JBS Jewish Blind Society
1 Craven Hill, London, W2
Tel: 01–262 3111

Jewish Blind Society (Scottish
Branch)
49 Coplaw Street, Glasgow, G42

Jewish Blind Society (Day Centre)
91–93 Stamford Hill, London,
N16 5SP
Tel: 01–800 5672

London Association for the Blind
14–16 Verney Road, London,
SE16 3D2
Tel: 01–732 8771

National Federation of the Blind
(Scotland)
Miss J Watt, 31–6 Pilrig Street,
Edinburgh EH6 5AR

National Library for the Blind
Cromwell Road, Bredbury,
Stockport, SK6 2SG
Tel: 061–494 0217

National Library for the Blind
(Braille, Moon and Large Print)
35 Great Smith Street, London
SW1P 3BU

North Regional Association for
the Blind
Headingly Castle, Headingly
Lane, Leeds 6
Tel: 0532–62666

Oculus — A monthly newsletter of
the Partially Sighted Society
40 Wordsworth Street, Hove,
Sussex, BN3 5BH

Optical Information Council
Walter House, 418–422 Strand,
London, WC2R OPB
Tel: 01–836 2323

Partially Sighted Society
40 Wordsworth Street, Hove,
Sussex, BN3 5BM
Tel: 0273–736053

Partially Sighted Society (Midlands
Office)
Breaston, Derby, DE73 UE

Radio London
35A Marylebone High Street,
London, W1
Tel: 01–486 7611

Royal Commonwealth Society for
the Blind
Commonwealth House,
Haywards Heath, Sussex

Royal London Association for the
Blind
105 Salisbury Road, London, NW6
Tel: 01–624 8844

Royal National Institute for the
Blind
224–6–8 Great Portland Street,
London, W1N 6AA
Tel: 01–388 1266

RNIB Library and Publications
Department
    338–346 Goswell Road, London,
    EC1V 7JE
    Tel: 01–837 9921

RNIB Moon Branch
    Holmesdale Road, Reigate,
    Surrey, RH2 OBA
    Tel: 07372–46333

RNIB Students Braille Library and
Students Tape Library
    Braille House, 338–346 Goswell
    Road, London, EC1V 7JE
    Tel: 01–837 9921 or
    01–278 9615

St Dunstans
    12 Harcourt Street,
    London, W1
    Tel: 01–724 3716

Talking Newspaper Association of
the UK
    84 Moorgate, London
    EC2M 6SQ

Torch Trust for the Blind
    Torch House, 4 Hassocks Road,
    Hurstpierpoint, Sussex
    Tel: Hallaton 301

Ulverscroft Press
    Station Road, Glenfield,
    Leicester, LE3 8BR

Warwickshire Association for the
Blind
    George Marshall Centre,
    Puckering's Lane, Warwick,
    CV34 4UN
    Tel: 0926–494129

## Publishers of Books in Large Print

Magna Print Books
    Magna House, Long Preston, Nr
    Skipton, N. Yorks, BD23 4ND
    Tel: 07294–225

Ulverscroft Large Print Books Ltd
    The Green, Bradgate Road,
    Anstey, Leicester
    Tel: 0533–365325
    (Also publish Hymn Books,
    Song Books and Accompaniment
    Books in large print).

Hymns Ancient and Modern Ltd
    St Mary's Works, St Mary's
    Plain, Norwich, NR3 3BH
    Tel: 0603–612914

Torch Trust (see above) also
    publish Hymn and Prayer Books

Music — DLF (see above) has a
    complete list of music publishers
    available on application

# INDEX